My Life, My Soul — Surviving, Healing And Thriving After An Abusive Relationship

Part 1: Surviving

Ivette Attaud

My Life, My Soul — Surviving, Healing and Thriving After An Abusive
Relationship — Part 1: Surviving

MLMS Publishing
50 Harrison Street, Suite 212 H
Hoboken, New Jersey 07030

Website: www.mylifemysoul.com
Email: ivetteattaud@mylifemysoul.com

Author photo by Michelle Wild — MWildphotography
Edited by Kip Smith
Indexed by Atlantic Authoring

ISBN-13: 978-0-615-44061-3 (MLMS Publishing)
ISBN-10: 0-615-44061-4
Library of Congress Control Number: 2011906149

This book is dedicated to all who have survived any form of abuse, as well as to those who have lost their lives, including my daughter Samantha Michelle.

Over twenty years ago, I stood at her grave on Fort Bragg and promised that one day I would make sure her death would not be in vain. Writing *My Life My Soul* is my way of keeping my promise so she can rest in peace.

Table of Contents

Preface

As of the completion of this book, it has been over twenty years since I buried my daughter in Fort Bragg's Main Post cemetery and left my abusive husband. Almost ten years ago, I started to write down my deepest thoughts, feelings and experiences from my teenage years all the way to adulthood as a way of coping with the loneliness and isolation that is all too familiarly felt by not only those still in abusive relationships, but also those who have left. As with anyone who has experienced relationship abuse, you remember everything — every act of violence, every cruel word, every scar, what made you cry, where you were and what you were doing when these things happened. Initially, these thoughts were written for four reasons:

1. as a way of coping with the loneliness, isolation and grief from losing my daughter;

2. I wanted something to pass down to my children so they would have a better understanding of what happened to me;

3. that my children would use my experiences as a guide to help them in their lives; and

4. to finally let go so I can move on.

With the exception of the only friend I had while living in North Carolina, no one, including my family, really understood what I went through. When I tried to reach out for help to report the abuse:

• The Military Justice System labeled me a troublemaker and didn't believe me;

• the Legal System called me a liar and jeopardized the safety of me and my children;

• the Mental Health System labeled me with Borderline Personality Disorder and joined the Legal System in jeopardizing the safety of me and my children;

• the Medical Community patched me up and sent me back home to my abuser;

• my own family refused to believe me and told me "my place was with my husband;" and

• my own church condemned me, telling me that what happened

to me was God's punishment for my sins.

These thoughts, feelings and emotions, in graphic detail, have turned into what you now hold in your hands. When I made the decision to publish this book and include actual documents as well as excerpts, I wanted:

- The Military Justice System to know what the daily reality of someone being abused by an active duty service member is like;
- the Legal System to understand that there is more to addressing the issue of domestic violence and abuse than "whoever gets to court first and has the most money wins,"
- the Mental Health System to see how their decisions and diagnoses, without the appropriate follow-up, severely impacts the lives of the victim and his or her children long after the case is closed;
- the Medical Community to see that the number of bruises and broken bones that pass through their emergency rooms are more than statistics;
- the Religious Community to realize that you have to heal the body before the spirit;
- people whose loved ones are in an abusive relationship to recognize the signs of the type of severe depression that leads to suicide and to understand that family support is crucial in the healing process;
- parents of teens who are dating to recognize the red flags of an abusive relationship; and
- anyone who currently is in an abusive relationship or has left an abusive relationship to know that you are not alone and you can and will break the emotional and psychological chains that bind you.

Just a few years ago, I founded My Life My Soul, The Unspoken Journey of Life After Domestic Abuse to raise awareness and foster a better understanding of domestic violence, as well as raise awareness about teen dating violence. When I have been invited to various events to talk about domestic violence and abuse, I was emotionally and spiritually moved by scores of men and women who have been brave enough to share their story with me.

As a former member of an organization that advocated for the rights of women and children, I came in contact with women who, as of a few years ago, had similar experiences. I have seen domestic violence laws evolve and change over the years, all designed to protect the rights of women and children. Yet thirty-two million men, women and children have experienced some form of physical violence, including sexual, emotional, psychological, financial or spiritual abuse. Some of those thirty-two million Americans have even lost their lives as a result, and those I will call the real victims.

In teen dating relationships, females aged 16 to 24 are more vulnerable to intimate partner violence than any age group. What is even more astounding is that 54% of parents admit they haven't spoken to their teen about dating violence.

Why is this happening? I believe that despite new laws being created to protect those who experience relationship abuse, a lack of coordinated resources, gender bias and prejudice is what enables millions of men, women, and children to fall through the cracks like my children and I did.

Without help from any of the systems designed to help those in abusive relationships, I had no other choice but to pull myself up by my bootstraps and move on because I didn't want to spend the rest of my life being angry, feeling isolated and ashamed of what happened to me. I wanted to be free from the emotional, physical and psychological chains of my abuser and move on to an improved way of living and a better quality of life for me and my children.

Deep down inside, a part of us wants to be happy and fulfilled. That healthy part of ourselves has been buried under years of neglect, abuse, criticism and other destructive forces. Change is never easy and it is always easier said than done, but a conscious effort to change has to be made in order to really know how enjoyable life can be after leaving an abusive relationship.

With inner strength and help from my Higher Power, I have learned to let go of the negativity in my life that weighed me down so I could move forward in a positive direction. Despite my physical and psychological scars, I have learned to love myself, embrace what has happened to me and hope that others can learn from my experience.

For anyone who has experienced abuse, surviving is not the first part of the healing journey — telling yourself you are a survivor is.

Your life and your soul depend on it.

Some names have been changed to protect the innocent and the guilty. Fictitious names are marked with an asterisk (*).

Acknowledgments

To my three children — you have been the light of my life, my core, my reason for surviving. There have been days that you have given me the strength to wake up and face my challenges, and I love all of you for that.

To Michael — thank you for your patience and your unwavering love.

To S. D. — thank you for always reminding me that there is light at the end of the tunnel.

To Kip Smith, my editor, and Atlantic Authoring — thank you so much for helping me with this difficult project.

Last, but not least, to my Higher Power — I couldn't have lived to tell my story if it weren't for you. You have carried me at times in my life when I felt I couldn't take another step.

Chapter 1

Fall 1983 — When We First Met

It was October 1983 when I first met him. At sixteen and in my junior year at Brooklyn Tech High School in New York, I was still a big kid at heart. Every winter, Bernice* and I looked forward to ice skating at Lasker Rink in Central Park because it was one of the few harmless activities our parents allowed us to do. The extent of my outdoor activities was limited to playing outside with the neighborhood kids, reading a book or going to the Kingdom Hall. My mom used to tell me as a kid that "Boys and books don't mix," so at the ages of fifteen and sixteen, my sister Bernice and I were not allowed to date. By the middle of the school week, my sister and I talked about going skating on Saturday in Central Park, what we were going to wear and reminded each other to make sure to clean and polish our ice skates. We even talked about decorating our skates, so we grabbed all of the red and blue yarn our mother had so we could make pom-poms. On Friday when Bernice and I came home from school, we were in a good mood because we knew we were going ice skating the next day. By the next morning, we were so excited that we completely forgot that we had to go out in field service, which meant we had to knock on doors and spread the word of God. That morning, preaching and going out in field service was the last thing on our minds because we wanted to eat breakfast, watch cartoons, put on our skates, go out and have some fun. But in our family, God always came first and we had to do what our parents told us to do, so Bernice and I went out preaching with our parents. We knew that if we didn't, we wouldn't be able to go skating later.

When we got home from preaching around midday, my sister and I ate lunch, quickly changed into our outfits, grabbed our skates, said goodbye to our parents and headed to the rink with a reminder from our mother that we had to be home by 7 p.m. We ran out of the apartment building we lived in on 111th Street and then walked across Central Park North and 110th Street and down the road towards the rink. As we climbed the steep hill and got closer, we heard the song "Maneater" by Hall and Oates blaring from the speakers.

". . .Oh here she comes,

Watch out boy she'll chew you up.

Oh here she comes,

She's a maneater . . ."

As we heard the music from the oversized speakers on top of the rink, it made us even more excited to get inside and start skating. After waiting in line for what seemed like an eternity just to pay to get in, we finally got inside and found a locker to put our shoes in after we changed into our skates. I got my skates on first and waited for Bernice to put on hers. We stood up and tried to keep our balance as we walked down the ramp and up to the ice. When we got to the edge of the rink, we watched people fly past us while we waited for our chance to get on. I got on first and held on to the rail and Bernice followed, holding onto the rail as well. I noticed some kids wore Bauer hockey skates, while others wore black or white figure skates. Bauer hockey skates were nice, but they were expensive and we knew our parents wouldn't have bought them for us. As soon as I saw an opening, I skated along the outside of the crowd and dared my sister to keep up with me. We skated for about an hour as we had fun listening to the music, when I told her I was getting off the ice to get something to eat from the concession stand.

Bernice loved french fries, so when I placed my order at the concession stand, I made sure to get enough so we could share. On my way back to the ice with the french fries and soda, I noticed that she was talking to a guy. From a distance, he looked to be about six-feet tall and light-skinned. As I got closer, I realized he wasn't a bad looking guy, except for the fact that he desperately needed a haircut and a tissue to wipe the caked snot from his nose. I was curious about the guy my sister was talking to, so I walked up to her and offered her some french fries. As I was about to say something to her, she interrupted me.

"Victor,* this is Ivette; Ivette, this is Victor."

Then she skated off and left me standing there looking really stupid. I couldn't believe she just set me up!

Victor and I stood on the ramp outside of the ice and talked for a bit, although I wasn't used to guys showing any interest in me whatsoever. I was very shy as a kid and always got picked on in school because of the way I looked. But, I enjoyed the attention nonetheless. We talked about the schools we went to, the kinds of classes we had, the teachers we didn't like. It turned out that he was the same age as me, lived a few blocks from us and went to a high school in midtown Manhattan which was the same school that my best friend went to. He mentioned he was in the Junior Reserve Officer Training Corps program in his high school. When I asked him what that was, he said it was a program that prepared him for going into the military when he graduated. I told him I was a Jehovah's Witness — nothing exciting there. He said he and his mother didn't like Jehovah's Witnesses and when they knocked on his door, he would turn his dog loose on them. His statement struck me as strange, so I asked him why he would be interested in me when he didn't like Jehovah's Witnesses. He told me that there was something "different" about me.

After finishing my fries and soda, I told Victor I was going back onto the ice to catch up with my sister. It wasn't long before Victor got on the ice and caught up with both of us. We skated for a few more hours, laughing, playing and watching Victor show off by doing fancy tricks on the ice in his Bauer hockey skates. We were having so much fun that it was almost 7 p.m. before we remembered we had to be home for dinner. So, we made our way off the ice towards the ramp and walked to our lockers so we could change back into our shoes and Victor followed us into the locker room as well. He gave me his home phone number and then he asked for mine. Again I told him I was a Jehovah's Witness, hoping that since he didn't like them, that he would change his mind. He insisted I take his number anyway and said that he only wanted to be friends. I was afraid to give him my home number because our mom didn't allow boys to call the house.

Secretly, I was excited at the prospect of having a boyfriend and it didn't matter to me that he wasn't a Jehovah's Witness. In my teenage mind, if a boy showed any interest in me, he wanted to be my boyfriend. As my sister and I left the rink and made our way back down the ramp out of Central Park, we talked about Victor and laughed at how he could have at least wiped the snot from his nose before he approached us. She told me there was something about him that she didn't like, and that for starters, he needed a haircut. Little did I know at the time that my sister would be on a long list of people who did not like Victor.

Later that week, I waited until our parents went to sleep and worked up the nerve to call Victor. His mother Susan* answered the phone and I politely asked for him, as I was taught to do by my parents when I called someone else's house. Then she screamed for Victor to pick up the phone. After a few minutes, he got on the phone and we continued our conversation from the weekend at the rink. In listening to him, I noticed that he liked to brag about the things he had and what his mother bought him — the latest this, the best that. He wasn't an only child; he had a six-year old sister from his mother's previous relationship. I found out years later that his mother had never married his father. Victor was the product of an affair between his 16-year old mother and his 35-year old father, who at the time, was married with six kids. When Susan got pregnant with Victor, his father left and went back to his wife and children in Colorado. He mentioned to me that his father never paid child support and when he left, his mother was so poor that she had to buy the most inexpensive meat from the supermarket. Victor resented him for that until the day his father drew his last breath.

It wasn't long before his mother picked up the other phone in the house and broke into our conversation.

"Victor, get off the goddamned phone!" I heard him sigh.

"Susan, I'm not done yet. I'll get off the phone when I feel like it!"

I was shocked! How could he talk to his mother like that? I thought that his response to his mother was a bit strange and disrespectful, because my sister and I could never have yelled at our parents or called them by their first names and live to tell about it! I found his self-confidence to be admirable, although at the time, I didn't know the difference between being cocky and being self-confident. I took the hint from his mother and told him I was getting off the phone and would talk to him later because I had homework to do. Besides, I didn't want to be the cause of an argument between him and his mother. His mother telling him to get off the phone with me was such a regular occurrence during our phone conversations that I could swear she didn't like me.

Victor and I talked on the phone everyday to the point that my mother noticed it and said something.

"Who are you talking to?" she asked.

"A friend from school," I replied.

"Why do you need to talk to your friend every night? Don't you see her every day in school?" She shook her head as she walked away from me.

Of course, my mother would think it was a girl I was talking to. When I spoke to Victor on the phone, I did everything I could to make sure she didn't find out that I was talking to a boy.

Victor surprised me one day by inviting me to his house to meet his mother. When I got there, Susan opened the door and when she did, I immediately sensed that she didn't like me. Their apartment was a two-bedroom in a high-rise pre-war building, a block away from Central Park on the west side of Harlem, with a doorman. Victor would always say that he didn't live in Harlem; that he lived on the "Upper West Side," as if "Harlem" was a curse word. Central Harlem begins at 110th Street at Central Park North, Spanish Harlem extends East Harlem's boundaries south to 96th Street, and the "Upper West Side" is between Central Park and the Hudson River and runs from 59th Street to 125th Street. I guess he felt living on the Upper West Side meant he lived in a better place than me. But that didn't matter, because to me, Harlem was and always will be my home!

Compared to where I lived with my family, their apartment was really small. The walls were painted an off-white color with brown carpeting on the floor. His mother's room was also small and cluttered while Victor slept in the master bedroom. His mother then turned the small living room into a bedroom for his little sister. The kitchen was even smaller, with just enough room to walk in, turn around and walk right out. I walked into the kitchen where Susan was and felt claustrophobic because I was used to our larger kitchen. I didn't say much while I was there, unless Susan asked me a question and I answered it. She seemed a bit crass, talking loud and fast and cursing like a sailor, which made me uncomfortable as well. I couldn't wait to leave and after about two hours, Victor offered to walk me home.

As we walked, Victor did most of the talking. Despite his unusual family life, Victor tried to impress me by telling me that his family had a lot of money. He talked about how his mother was driven home from work every night in a limousine and she would give him money to buy expensive things. From the perspective of a teenager, I didn't care about that because he was confident in ways that I wasn't and that was one of the things that made him attractive to me.

A couple of weeks later, I was working on a book report for school that was due the following week and planned a trip to the library on 115th Street to do some research. Victor told he had a book report to do too, so I suggested that we make a date and go to the library together. He told me he couldn't, that he had a part-time job after school and wanted to know if I could do the research for him. At the time, I really didn't see a problem with it and I liked him, so I said I would do it. Besides, I couldn't think of a reason not to do it. Later in the week, I went to the library and not only did I do the research for my book report, but his too. When I got back home from the library, I called the pizza shop where he worked to let him know he could pick up the research. His response shocked me.

"Thanks for doing the research for me, but I don't have time to write it. Could you write it for me?"

How could he have the nerve to ask me something like that? How was he managing his school work before I came along? My parents always taught us to work hard, do our homework, take responsibility for our own work and get good grades. I wasn't confrontational as a kid, always did what was asked of me and wasn't taught how to say "no." After arguing back and forth, I finally gave in and said I would write the report for him. Looking back, I guess I did that because I really wanted him to like me. I managed to write the report and get it to him so he could hand it in. When he did, his teacher suspected nothing and gave him (or should I say me) an "A" on the report.

I really liked Victor and wanted to introduce him to my parents but was nervous about the idea. As a Jehovah's Witness, you were taught that when you date, you should be ready to get married. If I introduced him to my parents, would they expect him to marry me? After thinking about it for some time, I finally got up the nerve to tell my mom about him. Of course she asked me if he was a Jehovah's Witness and I told her "No." Then she surprised me by inviting him to our house for dinner! My mom continued to ask me more questions about Victor: where he lived, went to school and how old he was. Although her questions were warranted, I was a bit apprehensive since that was the first time I actually talked to her about a boy I liked. She even agreed to cook one of my favorite meals, which was fried chicken, red rice, collard greens, potato salad and iced tea. Excited, I called Victor to invite him over to our house that weekend and told him what we were having for dinner. He sounded excited about it too and said he would be there.

My mother was from South Carolina and therefore from the very "old school" and that meant instilling in us the traditional female roles.

"You have to learn how to cook, clean and keep house. Men don't want no woman who can't cook and clean and keep house."

Between what my mother instilled in me and being raised as a Jehovah's Witness, where the wife's place was to be subservient to her husband, I had no reason to believe anything was wrong with that belief system. What reinforced my belief system was that within the Jehovah's Witnesses organization, only men could hold leadership positions in the Kingdom Hall and the women's role was to support them. I wanted to show Victor that I could be a good wife, so in anticipation of Victor's coming over later that day, I picked a room to clean and asked my sister to help me. She protested the whole time, mumbling under her breath so our mother wouldn't hear.

"Why do I have to help you? He's not MY boyfriend."

Like most siblings, I had to bribe her by giving up some of my allowance so she would shut up and help me.

My younger sister and I were born in the mid-60s and raised in Harlem. We lived on 114th Street between Lenox Avenue and St. Nicholas on the fifth floor of a tenement. My mother lived there for quite some time before we were born, having moved to New York from South Carolina in the 1950s and living with my grandmother's sister Eve.* My mother had three children that she raised while she lived in that apartment long after she and her first husband divorced. It was a spacious apartment with three bedrooms, a formal dining room with French doors and a long hallway. Our living room was a decent size, with 70s style multi-colored furniture covered in plastic and a multi-colored brown shag rug on the floor. We also had a floor model television along with a big cabinet that contained a record player and in order to play records, you had to lift the top off the whole cabinet. The kitchen was large enough for a kitchen table, washing machine, china cabinet, plenty of walking room and even a small walk-in pantry right off the kitchen where my mother kept the food. The bathroom was a decent size as well with a large, deep, white clawfoot bathtub. After divorcing her first husband, she eventually met and married my father who came to New York from Guadeloupe, French West Indies. I was born first and my sister followed eighteen months later. We lived there until I was thirteen years old, when developers came and moved everyone out so they could demolish the buildings and make way for a new high-rise apartment building. Today, the Harlem of my childhood is gone, with its mom-and-pop stores and other small businesses and was replaced by high-priced, high-rise apartment buildings and chain stores.

At the time, my mother wasn't too happy about leaving that apartment, not only for the years of memories there, but also that her rent was only $42.55 a month! Eventually, she and my father found an apartment on 111th street, across the street from Central Park right at the corner where St. Nicholas meets Lenox Avenue. The new apartment was just as big as our old one and even better that it was on the first floor. Bernice and I really liked the new apartment, with its fifteen-foot ceilings, hardwood floors, unusually tall windows and big rooms. It was when I had a scarf tied around my head, on my hands and knees scrubbing the hardwood floor with a brush and a bucket of water to prepare for Victor's visit, that I actually resented living in such a big apartment.

Victor was going to be there soon, so I yelled at Bernice to hurry up and finish cleaning. While I took the floor through another rinse, or "rinch" as my grandmother would say, I thought about whether my parents would like him or not. Just as I was drying the floor, the door bell rang. I panicked because I didn't have enough time to change my clothes, so I bit the bullet and went to answer the door dressed as the house slave. As I opened the door, the smell of fried chicken blew right past me and hit Victor in the face. He was about to walk in, but had to steady himself first because he laughed at how I was dressed. I called him stupid in return and told him I was dressed like that because I was cleaning the house. I guess he didn't know about "gettin' down" and cleaning like that. I ignored his laughing as we walked down the hallway towards the kitchen where my mom put the finishing touches of sliced boiled egg and paprika on top of the potato salad. When I called out to her, she turned around and I introduced her to Victor. He was very respectful to her as he shook her hand and said hello. When he did that, she looked at me with a wide-eyed look and I could tell by that look that she was glad he was well-mannered, even though he wasn't the same religion as me. We continued walking down the hallway through the dining room into the living room, where my dad relaxed on the couch, watching television and drinking his favorite Reingold beer. I introduced Victor to my father and he shook his hand as well. My father wasn't as strict about religion as my mother was and thinking back to that time, I don't think he cared too much for it because he was born a Catholic and when he met my mom, he converted to a Jehovah's Witness. Victor and I sat on the couch and watched TV with my dad while we waited for the food to be done. Unlike me, Bernice had time to change out of her house clothes and put on something more presentable before she came into the living room to say hi to Victor. Another ten minutes went by before my mother came into the living room and told us the food was ready. In reinforcing traditional female roles, my mother fixed my dad's plate and then asked me if I would fix Victor's plate. Victor seemed surprised that my mom served my dad first, but that was how we did things at home. Bernice fixed her plate, then I fixed Victor's plate and we all sat down at the dining room table to eat. When Victor saw the fried chicken, red rice, collard greens and potato salad on his plate, he slowly pushed the plate away as if he didn't want to eat it.

"I'm sorry ma'am, but I don't eat yellow potato salad."

My mother raised one eyebrow in disbelief at what he said.

"What do you mean, you don't eat yellow potato salad? Don't you eat potato salad at home?"

"Yes I do ma'am, but the potato salad my mother makes is white."

"Victor it's the mustard that makes it yellow," my mother said, as if that was something he should have already known.

He turned up his lip and said his mother never put mustard in her potato salad, that hers was white. My mom was shocked because being from the South, she never knew potato salad to be made any other way than with mustard.

She put her hands on her hips and said "Just try it."

He tried it and he liked the food so much that before long, his plate was clean. We stayed at the table and talked and laughed for a quite a while before it was time for Victor to go home. As he was leaving, he told my parents he enjoyed the food and had a good time. I walked him to the door, kissed him goodbye and said we would talk later. As I walked back down the hallway, I got the feeling that Victor was a little uncomfortable with us sitting at the table as a family, as if he wasn't used to that.

As Christmas was right around the corner, Victor called to say that he wanted to see me on Christmas Eve and that he had a surprise for me. I was excited at the prospect of getting a gift from him because it was the first time a boy had given me something, and that made me feel very special. When Victor came to visit me on Christmas Eve, he gave me a small box covered with Christmas wrapping paper. Inside was a writing pen with blue ink that smelled like perfume. It was a small, inexpensive gift, but I cared more about the fact that he gave me something than how much it cost. Although I was not raised to be materialistic, I noticed that Victor spent a lot of money on himself, but when it came to spending money on others, he was cheap.

For several months, Victor and I were like most teenage boyfriends and girlfriends, talking on the phone until late at night during the week and seeing each other on the weekends. We didn't really go out on "dates" per se, but he would either come by the house or he, my sister and I would spend time together walking our two Chihuahuas in Central Park. My mom once told me that she would rather have Victor come to the house to see me than my "going out in the street" to meet him. It was fun being around him and for a while, our relationship didn't go passed kissing because I didn't want the relationship to go any further. I didn't know anything about sex and conversations with my mother about sex, dating and relationships were pretty much short and sweet because she was uncomfortable talking about it. Instead, she made short, clipped statements such as:

"Boys and books don't mix."

"A man only wants you for one thing and, once he gets what he wants, he'll dump you."

"You give him what you got between your legs and once he gets it, he'll take advantage of you."

"You have to learn how to cook, clean and keep house because a man won't want you if you don't."

Talk about confusing! But I guess those were the life lessons my mother learned and thought the only thing left to do was to pass them on to us.

One day, Victor suggested we play hookey from school and I come over to his house, with the reassurance that his mom would be at work. I was a "good little girl" and never played hookey before, but the thrill of getting caught would be fun, so I agreed to go to his house. He told me he made an arrangement with the doorman to ring the apartment bell if his mother came home early and that would give him enough time to get me out of the house. Being naïve and a virgin, I thought that we would hang out and talk, as having sex was the last thing on my mind because I was taught that you don't have sex until you're married. But when I got there, we ended up having sex after all. Afterwards, Victor called me his "little virgin" and said those three words that every young woman wants to hear from her boyfriend — I LOVE YOU.

Afterwards, as I lay in the bed with Victor, I thought to myself that having sex with him was okay since we were dating. He said he loved me so that meant it would only be a matter of time before he asked me to marry him, right?

I didn't realize at the time how having a romanticized view of my relationship with Victor would severely distort my judgment.

Chapter 2

Spring 1984 — Young Love

Dating Victor made me feel like a grownup and it was nice to have someone care about me. I liked Victor because he was confident, or so I thought, and his mother let him do a lot of things that my mother wouldn't let me do. Growing up, my parents never told me that one day I would fall in love. I wasn't taught about what being in love feels like, or that there was a big difference between liking someone and loving them. So I thought that what transpired between Victor and me was normal. Although we didn't do things like go to the movies or go out to eat, it was nice to have someone other than my parents to show me affection.

After dating for a while, Victor became preoccupied with the idea that I was cheating on him. Although I reassured him I wasn't, I also noticed that he never volunteered any information as to whether he was faithful to me or not.

"You wouldn't cheat on me, would you Ivette?"

"No, Victor. I would never cheat on you." And that was the extent of those conversations.

Victor told me once that he knew a few guys that went to my high school and although I asked who they were, he never revealed their names to me.

"That's not for you to know," he would say.

Sometimes, he would ask me about what happened at school just to see if I was telling him the truth or not. I thought it was because he wanted to know how my day went, but this was a red flag that I should have paid attention to, but didn't.

Victor came to my house one day after I got home from school.

"I heard you were talking to some guy today. What's his name?" Victor asked, as if he couldn't remember the guy's name.

"What are you talking about?" I replied.

I quickly thought back on everything I had done that day. I didn't see anything wrong with what he asked me, since he was my boyfriend and felt he had a right to ask me those type of questions. Since Victor was familiar with the teachings of Jehovah's Witnesses, he knew that a man couldn't date you unless he had plans to marry you. So, it felt like the normal course of the relationship to assume that since we dated and started having sex that Victor would eventually marry me. I was also preoccupied with wanting to prove to him that I was capable of being a good wife and that I was an honest person, so I didn't mind telling him what I did during the course of the day.

"I stopped and talked to this one and that one. What are you saying?" I asked him.

"I'm saying I don't want you talking to any guys. It makes me angry when you talk to other guys. My friend knew who you were and told me he saw you talking to some guy on the football team."

Victor was right about that because I did talk to a guy who was in my class and was on the football team. It upset me that he had someone spying on me and although I asked him who this "friend" was, Victor never did tell me. It wasn't long before I started to feel isolated and uncomfortable talking to anyone in school because whoever this "friend" was, he was reporting everything I did back to Victor. I didn't think it was fair that Victor knew what I did in school but didn't volunteer any information about his daily activities. My instincts told me that something with Victor wasn't quite right. When I was a teenager, I didn't know what "instincts" were, but learned the hard way that I should always trust them. So, I called my friend Maxine,* who was my best friend since we were in first grade. We both went to the Kingdom Hall, always went to each others' houses and our parents knew each other as well.

"You've seen Victor at school, right?" I asked her.

"Yeah, I've seen him at school," she replied.

"Have you seen him talking to other girls?"

"I'm not sure," she replied.

I told her about the conversation Victor and I had earlier. I got the feeling that she didn't like him and saw what he did in school, but didn't want to tell me. Then she came up with an idea.

"You could sneak into my school. I know where a couple of Victor's classes are and you don't need identification to get in. I know a few of the security guards and a side door you could sneak into."

Perfect! I'll sneak into Victor's school and see who HE'S talking to! Maxine and I talked about the details of the plan — what day, what time and how we would do it. The only thing I didn't know was where I was going to go after that! I couldn't stay in her school all day!

The day came for me to sneak into Victor's school and spy on him. Maxine let me in the side door like she said she would. It was fun ducking in and out of stairwells and trying not to get caught by the school's security guards. When Maxine showed me where Victor's class was, we snuck up to a corner in the hallway and were startled by a thundering male voice that nearly shook us out of our skins.

"What are you girls doing in the hallway?"

The voice came from a school security that was behind us. That's it — I'm going to get arrested for trespassing. How am I going to explain this episode to my parents? I thought. But Maxine was a little more quick-thinking than I was.

"She's new in school, so I was just showing her around," she said to him.

To keep us from getting in trouble, Maxine laughed and flirted with the security guard. Then she walked back towards me.

"It's okay, he's not going to bother us."

I was glad that Maxine distracted the security guard so I wouldn't get kicked out of the school and arrested for trespassing. We hung out for the rest of the day while she skipped classes to help me find the next place to hide. Maxine took me to an empty classroom where I could hide for about half an hour until school was over. She told me she had to hand in homework for one of her classes and would meet me in the empty classroom, which was across from where Victor's Jr. ROTC class was. Victor didn't know that Maxine and I were best friends and I wanted to keep it that way. If he could have a spy in my school, I could have one in his! When she came back to the classroom, we peeked through the window of the closed door and giggled when Victor showed up. Then we watched as he talked to other junior recruits in his class when a girl walked up to Victor and gave him a kiss! Maxine and I stopped giggling and looked at each other.

"Do you know who that bitch is?" I asked Maxine.

"I sure do. Her name is Maxine too. Maxine Williams."* Gotcha! I thought as I turned to Maxine.

"If he thinks he can watch what I do so he can do what he wants, he's crazy!"

At that moment, I thought that Victor was really stupid for wanting to keep tabs on me and not thinking for one moment I might be keeping tabs on him! We watched as Victor talked with the other Maxine for a bit, then he took her around the corner from the classroom and they kissed some more! The sight of watching him with someone else was unbearable. I wanted to run out of my hiding space and punch that girl and Victor in the face! Maxine must have sensed what I was going to do because she grabbed my arm.

"Ivette, don't do that now! Wait until Victor gets to your house, then confront him!"

What Maxine said made sense. I decided to be patient and wait until Victor got to my house. Then, I was going to break up with him.

Victor came to my house a couple of days later. As I let him in through the door, he tried to kiss me and I turned my cheek.

"Don't kiss me!" I said to him under my breath.

I walked away from him towards the living room and sat down.

"What's wrong with you, Ivette?"

He acted as if he did nothing wrong. After being with Victor for a while, I got to know that look — it was as if part of him was surprised and part of him tried not to laugh. I couldn't hold it in anymore, so I came right out with it.

"Who is Maxine?"

"Who?" he asked sheepishly. I started getting mad all over again.

"Maxine? Maxine your friend?" he replied.

Geez, how did he know that Maxine and I were friends? That's when I remembered my friend's name was the same as his other girlfriend. I ignored his question.

"I HEAR you and Maxine are real lovey-dovey these days!" I yelled at him.

Victor had a surprised look on his face before he raised his voice.

"How DARE you accuse me of messing around with your friend!"

I put my hand in his face to stop him from talking.

"MAXINE WILLIAMS, YOU ASSHOLE! Don't act like you don't know what I'm talking about! You didn't have a problem with someone spying on me in my school and reporting back to you. Only thing is, I SAW you and Maxine kissing!"

Victor's facial expression changed and the color in his face reddened.

"You couldn't have seen me and Maxine kissing! I bet your slut friend Maxine told you!" He was so angry he looked like he wanted to hit me.

"No, Victor, I saw you with my own eyes! You know what, you make a choice. It's either me or Maxine!"

Victor had a habit of lying, even when the truth was presented to him. I wanted Victor to leave right then and there, but instead, he sat down on the couch as fake tears welled up in his eyes.

"You don't have the right to spy on me! Maxine is just a friend!" He said.

He didn't believe that I actually saw him. I wasn't about to tell him how I got into his school. That would be my little secret. Victor continued talking through his fake tears.

"I can't believe you don't trust me! I love you! You're my little virgin! I don't know what I would do if I lost you!"

I stared at Victor. I felt my anger subside as he sat on the couch with tears streaming down his face while telling me how much he loved me. By saying that, Victor turned the tables and shifted the blame on me. Then, while tears welled up in my eyes, I actually felt ashamed for accusing Victor in the first place. After a brief thirty-minute breakup, Victor and I were together again.

Chapter 3

Summer 1984 — The First Time

It wasn't until my grades slipped and I was in danger of not graduating from high school that I realized how preoccupied I was with Victor. Because everything between us happened so gradually, I couldn't see that I was vulnerable to being manipulated and controlled by him. So, I spent my last semester in high school going to day school, night school and summer school just to graduate on time. As I signed up for summer school, I could hear my mother's voice in my head: "boys and books don't mix."

It was almost June and our respective proms were right around the corner. I was so sure Victor would take me to my prom but, to my disappointment, he never asked. So, I decided I would go to my prom alone and waited a few weeks for my mom to mention it, but she never did. I got tired of waiting because the money for the prom was due soon, so I approached her while she washed dishes.

"Ma, can I go to my prom?" I asked, then waited nervously for her to answer.

"What day is it on?" she asked.

I had a sinking feeling in my stomach. I knew what she was leading up to.

"Wednesday," I said in a mumble.

"You know we go to the Kingdom Hall on Wednesday nights. You don't have any business going to your prom and listening to that worldly music and that will interfere with you serving the Lord! And nothing should come between you and the Lord!"

I walked away from her with tears in my eyes. Why couldn't I do things like other kids? Not being able to go to my prom because I had to go to the Kingdom Hall was one of many things from my childhood that haunted me as an adult.

Feeling depressed, I called Victor's house to see if he was still going to his prom, but he wasn't there and Susan picked up the phone instead.

"Victor's not here Ivette. He ran to the store for me. Wait a minute, he just came in the door. Victor, go and try on the tux I just bought for you. I'll talk to Ivette while you try it on."

In the meantime, Susan and I made small talk. I heard Victor protesting in the background about trying on the tux.

"Come in here and let me see you," Susan yelled at Victor.

"Damn, he looks good, Ivette. I think I'm going to have to take his pants back to the store and exchange them for a larger size. They're so tight you can see how big his dick is!"

Susan laughed hysterically, but I didn't think a comment like that was funny. Susan had no boundaries to what she said and did, and in turn, Victor didn't have any boundaries either. Then I knew where Victor got his warped sense of humor from. I pulled the phone away from my ear and stared at it as I thought that there was something wrong with that woman to talk about her son like that. I didn't like it when Susan got a kick out of cursing like a sailor just to shock me. I didn't like her language because we didn't talk like that at my house, but for her and Victor, it was normal. I couldn't take listening to her anymore, so I told Susan to have Victor call me when he was done. Besides, it was getting more and more upsetting for me to know I wasn't going to the prom and he was.

When Victor called back some time later, I asked if I could see him the next day which was Saturday, and he agreed to come by. I thought I would cheer myself up by spending some time with him, so when we went out on Saturday, we talked about our plans after high school. Brooklyn Tech was a prestigious college-bound high school and I went there not because I wanted to, but because I passed the test. I come from a generation where a high school diploma was all you needed to get a good job and my parents did not encourage us to further our education. What was worse was that Jehovah's Witnesses frowned upon anything that would "interfere with serving the Lord," including going to college. Victor, on the other hand, wanted to go into the military since he really liked being a part of Jr. ROTC in high school. After he got out of the military, he said he wanted to be a police officer. I told him that my immediate plans entailed graduating high school and getting a job. We talked for a while in the park and shared ideas about our plans for the future. It was a warm sunny day and we saw people walking their dogs, people playing loud music on their boom boxes, some rode their bikes while others jogged or played with their kids in the park. The ice skating rink where we first met was used as a pool in the summertime and Victor and I sat on a bench near the entrance to the pool. We stood up and watched as the workers swept, painted the pool and removed the rubber flooring left from the winter. I let my dogs off their leashes so they could run around while Victor and I talked, when in the middle of my saying something, he hauled off and slapped me so hard that he knocked my earring out of my ear. My face stung and while I stood there dumbfounded, I wondered how he could have the nerve to hit me like that. As he stared at me, I noticed his eyes darting to the left and right as if he was checking to see if someone was watching him. Then, out of the blue, he screamed to the top of his lungs.

"Don't you ever fuckin' talk to me that way! Ever!"

My two Chihuahuas, being so protective of me, ran towards Victor and barked at him because they heard his yelling. With the left side of my face still stinging, I turned slowly to look in the direction he looked in and saw a couple of guys within earshot of us. They looked at us and turned away as if acknowledging that what Victor had done was right.

"Now pick up your goddamned earring!" he screamed.

I knew Victor liked to show off but this was ridiculous! Still holding my face and fighting back tears because I was angry, I quickly assessed the situation and what Victor was trying to do. He was showing off for those guys and I was sure he didn't even know them! I couldn't understand why Victor felt he had to prove his manhood to those strange men by hitting me in the first place. I should have seen this as a sign that Victor had the capacity to be an abuser when he became an adult.

Then he repeated himself.

"Pick that shit up, I said!"

I bent down to pick up my earring and as I began to stand up, I curled my right hand into a fist and shot it straight up into Victor's chin.

"How dare you fuckin' hit me!" I said to the top of my lungs.

I wasn't taught to fight but I was definitely taught how to defend myself. Victor stood there shocked as he held his bloody mouth because when I punched him in his chin, he bit his tongue. He was so shocked that I hit him back that he couldn't talk. Then I continued to yell at him.

"Nobody hits me! You are NOT my father and my father NEVER laid a hand on me! I don't ever want to see you again, you fuckin' asshole!"

By then my dogs were getting out of control, as they barked and jumped around because we were fighting. I managed to get them calmed down enough to put them back on their leashes and walked out of the park towards my house. I walked past those same guys that saw Victor hit me and hoped they might have said "that wasn't right," or "he shouldn't have done that." But instead, they said nothing.

Victor followed me and called for me to stop.

"Ivette, stop! Wait a minute! I'm sorry! I didn't mean to hit you!"

What in the Hell was he thinking? He hits me then says he's sorry? I came to the conclusion that Victor was testing the waters to see if he could get away with hitting me.

His pleas fell on deaf ears as I stormed down the ramp and out of the park. Victor caught up with me and grabbed my arm as he tried to keep me from walking any further.

"Ivette, I'm very sorry. I don't know what happened."

"You hit me! That's what happened! You didn't have any right to hit me. I didn't do anything to you!" I yelled at him.

Victor continued to plead with me. "I'm sorry Ivette, please don't leave me."

I snatched my arm away from him and continued walking when he grabbed me by the arm again and tried to kiss me. I was so disgusted that I pushed him away. Then he laughed and rubbed his chin.

"I gotta tell ya though — you've got one hell of a right hook!"

What was wrong with this guy to think that hitting me was funny? I ignored him as I continued to walk towards my house with him following me all the way to my building. I told him again that I didn't want to see him anymore and went inside my house, leaving him standing on the stoop. Once I got inside, I let the dogs off their leashes and went to my room. Then I plopped down on my bed, still reeling from everything that happened. I decided not to tell anyone about that incident — not even my mother.

I was conflicted as to whether I should forgive Victor or not, because his actions didn't make sense to me. Part of me didn't want to be with him anymore and part of me thought that this was an isolated incident — after all, he did apologize for hitting me. Is this how someone treats you when they like you? Hit you then say "I'm sorry?" In my head, I made excuses for Victor. There was no one I could talk to about what he did to me, at least no one that I could trust. I was determined not to have any more to do with Victor, but for several days, he called me to beg my forgiveness and wore down my resolve in the process. So, I eventually forgave him. It never occurred to me at that time that Victor's actions were a prelude to worse things that were to come.

As the summer wound down, I finished summer school, passed all my classes and received my diploma. Victor, on the other hand, was packing to go to Basic Training at Fort Dix in New Jersey for nine weeks. During that time, we talked constantly on the phone, and he asked me over and over again not to cheat on him while he was in Basic Training.

"I'm going to need you to be there for me because Basic Training is hard. Please don't cheat on me. I love you and you will always be my little virgin. It would be hard for me to concentrate on finishing Basic Training if I thought you were cheating on me."

I had such a romanticized view of my relationship with Victor that I couldn't see the forest for the trees. I thought it was romantic that he told me he loved me and it made me feel special. I also felt that I needed to prove to him that I would make a good wife because that's what I was raised to do — to be a good wife. It never occurred to me why Victor was so preoccupied with my cheating on him and made me responsible for what he could or couldn't do.

I felt good knowing that he needed my help to get him through Basic Training, so I assured him I would stay faithful to him. I had mixed feelings at the time because I was sad that he was leaving, glad he told me he loved me, yet still mad at him for hitting me weeks earlier. He promised he would call me as much as he could. When Victor left for Basic Training in August, I focused on finding a job so I wouldn't be depressed about being without him.

Chapter 4

Fall 1984 — A Long-Distance Relationship

Shortly after I graduated high school, I found a job working in the children's clothing department at Lerner's Home Office. My 18th birthday was in a couple of weeks and, like most teenagers, thought something "magical" would happen when I woke up that day. But, nothing special happened — I just got up and went to work.

After nine long weeks, Victor finished Basic Training and Susan, his little sister and I traveled on the bus to Fort Dix for his graduation. The graduation ceremony was nice, where trainees were dressed in their military uniforms and performed fancy marches and synchronized gun drills to entertain their families and friends. After the graduation, we went to the mess hall and ate lunch as Victor told us stories about what happened while he was in Basic Training, including a guy who committed suicide because he couldn't take all the stress. During lunch, Victor informed us he was allowed to come home for a few days after graduation, which made me happy. Afterwards, he had to report for his Advanced Individual Training at Fort Benning in Georgia, where he would learn combat skills and how to be a soldier. After we finished eating, we got on the bus and went back to New York. Victor went home with his mother and sister and I went to my house, feeling left out because I wasn't invited to spend the day with him and his family, but I didn't say anything to him about it. I just went home, watched TV and kept myself busy so I wouldn't think about Victor leaving again. Later that evening, Victor called and promised he would come by to see me. That lifted my mood, even if I was only going to see him for a little while.

When I was a teenager, it never occurred to me to date other guys just to be sure that Victor was the right person for me. I felt that if I dated someone else, I would be cheating on him and that was a mindset I would come to regret later in my life. When Victor came by, he surprised me with a marriage proposal. It wasn't romantic with his getting down on one knee and proposing with an engagement ring in hand. Just a simple, "Would you marry me?" was all he said. I excitedly said yes and when we talked about setting a date, he told me he wanted to wait until after he finished his training. I was so happy at that moment that I wasn't the slightest upset that he didn't give me an engagement ring. I told him I was going to tell my parents, but he asked me to hold off and wait until he left New York before I said anything.

When Victor left my house, I went to bed in a good mood and dreamed about my wedding day. I thought about the kind of gown I would wear, what my colors would be and which friends I wanted in my wedding party. And more importantly, I thought about how I was going to break the news to my parents. At that time, I felt that Victor abandoned me because he wasn't going to be there with me when I told my parents. The next day, while still in a good mood, I finally told them. My father was happy but my mother clearly was not.

"He's not in the same religion as you. You know what the Bible says about being unevenly yoked!"

Jehovah's Witnesses were taught that you couldn't marry someone who didn't practice the religion.

My mother could tell by my reaction that I was determined to marry Victor no matter what she said.

"Since it seems I can't talk you out of this and this is what you want to do, I'll support you," my mother reluctantly said.

While Victor was in Georgia, he called me whenever he could, albeit collect. I always accepted the charges, oblivious as to how expensive those calls were. Even so, I never complained about giving my mother upwards of $200 a month out of my paycheck for the calls. Victor never offered to reimburse me for the phone calls, and it didn't bother me because I was too excited about the wedding to let that spoil my good mood. When we had a chance to talk, we finally agreed on July 31, 1985 as our wedding day. Correction, I mostly talked about the wedding and he just listened. I talked about wedding colors, invitations, the guest list and everything else I had to do, but he didn't seem so interested. Some years earlier, I had received a small settlement from a car accident, and it was enough money to buy everything I needed for the wedding. At one point in the conversation, I asked him what kind of tuxedo he wanted to wear and, without any emotion in his voice, he told me he was wearing his uniform.

Then the subject of money came up. I asked him if he had money to send me so I could pay for the wedding invitations.

"Why? Are you marrying me for my money? Because if you are, then we can call this wedding off right now!"

I pulled the phone away from my face and stared at it. Why would he say something like that to me? For Victor to think I was marrying him for his money was an insult and I told him so.

"If you think I'm marrying you for your money, you are sadly mistaken. You don't HAVE any money. Besides, I'm not getting married by myself and I shouldn't be the only one spending the money. YOU asked me to marry you, not the other way around!"

After saying that, I felt guilty for even asking for money for our wedding in the first place. After I got off the phone with Victor, it bothered me that I spent more time talking about the wedding than he did. I dismissed my feelings and to revive my good mood, focused on planning my wedding. Being a teenager and inexperienced with love and relationships, this was one of several red flags that indicated I shouldn't have married Victor in the first place and I completely ignored them.

Chapter 5

Spring 1985 — To Have And To Hold:
Maybe, Maybe Not

Our wedding was in a couple of months and I had finalized all of the arrangements. The wedding was going to take place in the Conservatory Garden in Central Park and, according to the news, the weather would be bright and sunny. We planned to have approximately sixty-five guests and Victor and I agreed that we would have a horse-drawn carriage carry us down Fifth Avenue towards the Garden. The wedding colors were ivory and dusty rose, from the bridesmaids gowns down to the invitations. Bernice's friend, Jasmine,* who studied to be a fashion designer in high school, designed my wedding gown and she was almost done putting it together. She designed a white, full-length gown made of lace and taffeta with a cathedral style train that was embroidered with white roses. The top of the gown had a sweetheart neckline with puffed sleeves that extended to a point at the hand and connected to my middle finger. All that was left to do was to design my headpiece and veil. My mother helped me to address and mail the invitations, which were ivory with a pearl embossed rose. I didn't have to worry about Victor's attire since he, his best man and groomsmen were going to wear their Army uniforms. Jasmine's father was a musician for Jazzmobile, which was a non-profit organization that produced world-wide jazz concerts and, as a wedding present, would handle all the entertainment. The reception was being held in a lounge in Harlem called Small's Paradise on 135th Street. My father, who was a chef, agreed to cater the wedding. Although Victor never sent me any money to plan the wedding, I thought I was once again proving myself to be the dutiful wife by handling and paying for our wedding, while my future husband was training to serve his country. I tried to see the glass as half-full instead of half-empty and understood that a marriage wasn't always 50-50, so I didn't see anything wrong with Victor not giving me money for the wedding. I was so busy with the wedding plans that I didn't realize several weeks had gone by before I next spoke to him.

When he called, I dominated the conversation, excitedly updating him on all the wedding plans. I was in the middle of asking him about the kind of food he wanted at the reception when he interrupted me.

"I don't want to get married."

Seconds went by before I could say anything.

"Why? What did I do? Do you realize I just sent out the invitations?" I added.

Then I got angry and was on the brink of tears. Before I could say anything else, Victor interrupted me.

"I just don't want to get married!" he yelled at me.

"I think you owe me an explanation!" I responded. Nothing but silence.

"I just had an appointment at the doctor and he told me I couldn't have kids," he said sadly.

Once again, silence. It took me a few seconds to process that information, since I always knew I wanted children. I sighed.

"Victor, it doesn't matter. We could always adopt."

That just seemed to make him angrier.

"The wedding's off and that's that. I don't want to talk about it anymore!"

By then, I couldn't control myself anymore and started to cry.

"Did I do something to upset you to make you not want to marry me?"

For a minute, I thought I heard a snicker but quickly decided that I was hearing things.

"No, I just can't have kids. Look, I'm really upset now. I'll talk to you later." Then he hung up.

The conversation lasted all of ten minutes and he didn't wait for me to say goodbye. He didn't say anything about the invitations that were mailed out or all the money that I spent; not so much as an apology. I fell on my bed, curled up into a fetal position and cried. Although my parents had a right to know that Victor just cancelled the wedding, I didn't want to tell them because I was too ashamed. Later on, when I was able to compose myself, I called Small's Paradise and informed them of the wedding cancellation and asked what their policy was. They told me it was too late to get a refund, so I basically lost my $1,500 deposit. I couldn't get a refund on my bridesmaids' gowns either.

It took me another two days before I could break the news to my parents. My mom didn't say much because the "I told you so" look on her face spoke in volumes and she just sighed.

"We have to call everyone and let them know the wedding is cancelled."

Then something dawned on me — I realized that all the people invited to the wedding were my family and friends! The only ones from Victor's side were his mother, sister and the guys from his unit that were going to be in the wedding! It was almost as if he didn't want a lot of people to know that he was getting married.

My mom got out her phone book and we took turns calling everyone to tell them the wedding was off.

At some point I knew I needed to call Susan to see if she could give me some insight as to why Victor would call off the wedding. I guess a part of me wanted to know if Victor was lying or not because I knew he liked to play mind games on people. When I called her, I cried when I told her about my conversation with him.

"Everything's going to be all right; just give him time." I composed myself to ask her the next question.

"Did he tell you what the doctor said about him not being able to have kids?" The phone was silent for a few seconds before she replied.

"No, he didn't tell me anything like that. Victor doesn't always tell me everything that's going on with him."

Little did I know I would eventually throw those words back in her face.

Again, I thought about that little snicker I thought I heard during my previous conversation with Victor, but couldn't be absolutely sure about it. Was this another one of Victor's games? Was she in on the game too and decided to lie to me to cover for him? It would be years later before I got the answers I looked for.

Still very much disappointed and hurt, I was eager to go back to work to get my mind off my troubles. Victor called a few days later out of the blue, which surprised me because I didn't expect to hear from him for quite a while. His tone was matter-of-fact and he talked as if everything was okay with us. I told him I didn't want to talk to him and hung up the phone. I did that a few times when he called and that happened for several days.

I slowly came to grips with the reality that Victor and I weren't getting married and the fact that I lost about $6,000 on a wedding that wasn't going to happen. Over the next few weeks, Victor's behavior continued to nag at me but I quickly put it towards the back of my mind. I wanted to focus on more positive things, as I was fresh out of high school and really wanted to be on my own. My parents didn't encourage us to further our education past high school and my religion frowned upon anything that would keep you from serving the Lord, so I made preparations to look for an apartment. The prospect of looking for an apartment and being on my own was exciting and after a while, I stopped thinking about Victor. I didn't want to concern myself with him because I wanted a good job, a decent relationship and my own place.

I knew I didn't want to live with my parents forever and felt independent enough that I could make it on my own. I even stopped talking to Susan and she did me a favor by not calling me. But something deep inside told me that she was doing what a mother does which was to cover up for her son, regardless of whether he was right or wrong. I thought that if I found my own place and moved out that I would eventually meet someone and start dating again.

Since I stopped calling Victor, his internal antenna must have alerted him to the fact that I was trying to move on with my life, so he came to my mother's house one day unexpectedly. He rang the bell and I went to open the door, not thinking it could have been him. He stood there and looked at me with this "I'm sorry" look on his face. For a minute, I tried to decide if I should let him in or not, so I stood in the doorway and asked him what he wanted. He asked if he could come in, looking like a little boy that got lost in a department store. Reluctantly, I let him in and closed the door. As I walked down the hallway, I yelled to my mom that Victor was there. When we walked past the kitchen where my mom and half-sister were talking, they stopped in mid-sentence to give Victor a perfunctory hello, which meant they were not happy with him for calling off the wedding. When we got to the living room, I sat down on the couch with my arms crossed defensively and Victor sat down on the loveseat opposite me.

"I know you don't want to talk to me, but just hear me out please. I've been thinking," Victor said. "I love you and still want to marry you."

I was speechless. Once again, what he said and what he did didn't match. I am finally starting to think more about myself and less about Victor, then he calls off the wedding less than two months ago, now this! Something didn't feel right about this and I was determined to find out what his angle was.

"What about what the doctor said about you not being able to have kids?" He cast his eyes down.

"The doctor made a mistake. He said I could have kids after all."

I really didn't know what to make of this latest development. How could a doctor make a mistake like that? I wasn't immediately overcome with excitement; instead I was again feeling that something was wrong with this situation, but quickly put the thoughts out of my mind. That was, until he asked for an answer right then and there. I let him know I wasn't ready to give him one.

"I think we should live separately on our own for a while. If you get out of the military and still want to get married, we can talk about it then. I'm in the process of looking for my own apartment."

When he lifted his head, he had a puzzled look on his face.

"What? Why do you want to have your own apartment?" he asked.

"Because I need my own space," I told him.

"Besides, when you come to New York, you can stay with me."

I felt like I was giving in to Victor by first not wanting anything to do with him, now telling him he could stay with me.

"It's not safe for a young woman to live by herself," he said.

Next thing I knew, Victor got up from the loveseat and called my mother and half-sister as he walked towards the kitchen, as if he didn't remember the cold shoulder they gave him when he first walked in.

"Did you know Ivette is talking about getting her own apartment and living by herself? Would you please tell her it's not safe for a young woman to live alone?"

I couldn't believe he was manipulating me through my family! Mysteriously, they seemed to forget about Victor calling off the wedding and my mother and older half-sister both agreed with Victor that I shouldn't have my own apartment. They walked into the living room with him right behind them. Then, my mother spoke.

"How are you going to pay your rent? Do you know all the things that can happen to a woman living by herself?" Victor stood behind them smiling.

I was really tired of being treated as if I didn't have any common sense or as if I was stupid. I felt that Victor was sabotaging my life and using my family to do it. I really wanted to be on my own and felt mature enough to make that decision for myself. I couldn't believe that they were trying to talk me out of moving out! What was I supposed to do? Live with my mother for the rest of my life? I just wanted to be independent!

After my mother and half-sister both pressured me into not moving out, they went back into the kitchen and continued their conversation. I stood there and glared at Victor while he talked to me.

"Can't you understand that I love you and don't want anything to happen to you? So much can happen to you if you were living alone and I don't know what I would do without you," as if telling me he loved me was going to cover up his manipulative tactics.

Everything happened so fast and I felt pressured by Victor and my family. First, my family made no bones about their dislike for Victor. Second, Victor called off the wedding. Third, my mother was the one who suggested I wait until Victor comes out of the military before we got married! Now, no one wants me to move out! I couldn't figure out why he didn't want me to live on my own since he was in the Army living his life and doing God knows what. But when he said he loved me, it made me feel like he truly cared about what happened to me.

"I need some time to think about this. You called off the wedding, now here you are just two months later and you want to get married again?" He shook his head in agreement.

"Yeah, that's it in a nutshell, but I don't want to tell anybody this time — let's elope. He said that in a low voice because he didn't want my mom and half-sister to hear. I'm going to be in New York for a few more days."

I was getting upset again. Why the rush? I felt the need to remind Victor yet again of what transpired over the past few months.

"You called off the wedding. You hurt me and I lost all of MY money! My family and I had to call everyone to tell them the wedding was off! You didn't contribute anything to OUR wedding. Why should I trust you? And, even worse, after all the hard and dirty work is done, you come back here wanting to marry me!" I screamed at him, finally unable to control my temper.

Victor tried to get me to lower my voice.

"I don't blame you for being angry. I was scared before, but I've had time to think things over and I want us to get married," he calmly said as he put his arms around my waist.

Oh how romantic! I just looked at him. Lord knows I wanted to be on my own and didn't want to be bothered with Victor anymore, but on the flip side, he did take my virginity. Who would want me after that? I took a deep breath and sighed.

"I'll let you know before you leave New York."

I went in my room to process what Victor had said and what I just did. I got mad at myself yet again for caving in. Why the quick turnaround? Why, after months of planning, he calls off the wedding only to want to elope less than two months later and couldn't come up with a logical explanation that I could accept? More importantly, why did he want to elope? I wanted to trust him, but a little voice inside of me said not to and definitely not to marry him. This would be one of many times I wished I had listened to that little voice inside me.

I called Victor the next day and told him I would marry him.

"Good! I'll come back by the middle of September and we can do it then. Only thing is, you can't move down here with me until I'm assigned to my Permanent Duty Station in North Carolina." I told him that was fine.

By the middle of September, like Victor promised, he came back to New York to see me. When he called, we talked about going to City Hall to get married on September 18th, two days after my birthday.

"Are you going to wear a suit?" I asked.

"No, I'm not going to wear a suit," he said.

Then we argued for a while about wearing a suit. The fact that we argued about what he was going to wear was yet another sign I should have paid attention to.

"Never mind," I finally said. I really didn't feel like arguing with him on the day that we were getting married.

I didn't feel as happy then as when I had planned the wedding on the original date. Since he didn't buy wedding bands and at that time I worked in the diamond district on 48th Street, I used my employee discount to buy the wedding rings. At the time, I didn't see anything wrong with buying the wedding bands, but once again, I was doing all the work and spending all the money. I was afraid to challenge him on the subject of wearing a suit for fear he would change his mind again about marrying me. To this day, I have tried to understand why I didn't push the issue of not wanting to marry him because all the signs were there. Little by little, the plans I had for myself got pushed into the background. I had no idea at the time that being in a relationship with someone meant that you didn't have to sacrifice your goals and dreams. If someone loves you, they should give you the space to grow as a person and not try to hold you back.

The next day, I called in sick and left the house as if I were going to work. I met Victor at the train station and we both got on the train to go to City Hall in downtown Manhattan. I wore a peach colored linen wrap dress with shoes to match. He wore a pair of Lee jeans and a plaid shirt. As we rode the train, I looked at what he wore and thought to myself that this man couldn't do so much as put on a decent suit to get married in! For a brief moment, I wanted to get off at the next stop, call the whole thing off and go home, but changed my mind because I thought it was too late to turn back. While on the train, we really didn't talk much or act like a happy couple eager to get married. Come to think of it, we really didn't look like we were together at all.

We finally got to City Hall, waited in line, got the application and filled it out. It was a short while before we were called to the judge's chambers.

"Are you sure you want to do this?" I asked.

"Yep," was all he said.

I secretly hoped he would change his mind because I didn't want to be the one to have a change of heart. Within minutes, it was done. We were pronounced husband and wife. No celebration, no people congratulating us, no fanfare, no gifts, no music, no first dance, no honeymoon.

We didn't do anything special after we were married — we got back on the train and went home. While on the train, I asked him if he was coming to my house so that we could tell my parents we got married.

"I've got to get back to my mother's house to start packing. You know I have to leave the day after tomorrow."

Okay, so he's leaving day after tomorrow, I thought. What did that have to do with today? Once again, I gave him one of those "I can't believe you're doing this to me again" looks. Instead of facing my parents together as a married couple, I had to face them alone and tell them what I did. When I told my parents, my mother lost her mind!

"WHAT!!!! What did you go and do that for, after that man called off the wedding and caused you to lose all your money?"

To this day, I don't know why my mother was surprised. I was in a religion that frowns on personal development, that teaches women to be good wives and mothers and support their husbands and then there's my mother, who did nothing but train me to be a good housewife. What was I supposed to do? What would she expect me to do but get married? Geez, I couldn't win!

She didn't hesitate to chastise me and make me feel like a two-year old who got caught with her hand in the cookie jar. My mother had a way of always making me feel like a child and it didn't stop, even when I became an adult.

"Ma, he said he was sorry for calling off the wedding," I responded.

Again, I found myself making excuses for Victor and justifying his behavior.

My father sat down, shook his head and said nothing because my mother said enough for the both of them.

"I don't know what possessed you to go and ruin your life like that, but what's done is done. Now, you have GOT to go and tell the elders at the Kingdom Hall what you did!"

Ruin my life? What made her think I was ruining my life? Did she REALLY think it was better for me to marry a man who was a Jehovah's Witness?

As a child, I remembered observing people in the Kingdom Hall — how they dressed, how they acted and how they treated my sister and me. Some had a standoffish attitude towards us, not even wanting their children to associate with us. But there was something I noticed that always stood out in my mind. I remembered going to service one night and seeing a woman with her husband and young son. The service was at night and I thought it was odd that she wore sunglasses. I also noticed she wasn't her friendly self, because she was unusually quiet. As I passed her after service and said "Hi" to her, I noticed that she was hiding a black eye behind her sunglasses.

When my mother blamed me for ruining my life, I paid her no mind. I came to the conclusion that marrying Victor was nothing compared to being married to someone in the Kingdom Hall who preached love and forgiveness and beat their wife.

For Jehovah's Witnesses, confessing to the elders is like going to confessional in a Catholic church. Only difference is, there is no anonymity. Everyone knows that you did something wrong when they see you talking to them.

As my mother continued talking, I thought to myself how everyone was trying to control my life. I was so wrapped up in my own thoughts that I tuned her out; she looked as if her mouth were moving but without sound. I'm eighteen years old and a grown woman — why do I have to tell anybody what I did, as if getting married were wrong? Why in the world did I have to confess and be judged by imperfect men who I knew were capable of abuse?

But, according to Jehovah's Witnesses, I committed a "sin" because I married someone who wasn't the same faith. So, I had to confess to the elders. Since when was it a sin to love someone? By telling the elders what I did, I was bound to be punished in some way. As a Jehovah's Witness, punishment for marrying someone outside of the faith depended on whether you are baptized or not. If you were baptized, then you could be excommunicated or "disfellowshipped" because you knowingly disobeyed God's laws. But since I wasn't baptized, I would be subjected to a lighter punishment and it would spare my mother the embarrassment of my being disfellowshipped.

To keep the peace because I was still living in my mother's house, I did what my mother told me to do. I had to go and tell the elders. She also asked me to invite Victor over to the house for dinner before he left to go back down South because she had some choice words for him and she wanted to say it to both of us.

The following night, I arrived at the Kingdom Hall just before service started. I pulled aside one of the elders and told him I eloped with someone who wasn't a Jehovah's Witness. I really resented spilling my business to imperfect men who would judge me. I didn't care that they were in charge of "keeping the congregation clean." At the end of the service, four of the elders got together in the office and called me in. I went in alone and sat in front of them. As they reminded me about being honest and telling the truth, basically trying to guilt me into telling the truth, I felt like I was in the Spanish Inquisition. They asked me all kinds of personal questions while they read scriptures to me.

"Did you have sex before you were married?" What difference did it make since I was already married?

"How long were you dating him?" Once again, what difference did it make? I was already married! But they felt I should have known better since I knew the "Truth," which were the teachings of Jehovah's Witnesses.

40

My Life, My Soul — Part 1: Surviving

I felt tortured with all their senseless questions and just wanted it to be over. About a half hour later, they asked me to step outside while they discussed what my fate would be. Ten minutes later, they called me back in the office.

"We have come to the conclusion that since you're not baptized, you won't be disfellowshipped. Instead, you will be marked and considered bad association. You can attend service but no one will be allowed to talk to you. You cannot make comments during service either."

What's the purpose of even going to the Kingdom Hall if no one can speak to me! What a crock! But I was glad that was finally over.

After getting home from the Kingdom Hall, I tried to forget about everything that happened and decided to call Victor.

"Ma wants to talk to us. Come over tomorrow for dinner."

"What does she want to talk to us about?" he asked.

"I dunno. Just come over." I responded.

The next day, when Victor came over for dinner, he looked scared because he didn't know what my mother was going to say to us. After dinner, we went to the living room where my mom and dad sat on the couch and Victor and I sat on the loveseat opposite them. My father didn't have anything to say and I really don't think any of this mattered to him, not because he didn't care, but because he really wasn't fanatical about religion like my mother was. Besides, my dad was always pretty easygoing. My mother pretty much dominated the conversation like she usually does.

"I can't believe you both went off and got married. You don't know anything about being grown and married, but I guess you got to grow up sometime. Victor, you married my daughter and I need you to remember that Ivette can't take too much stress."

Why in the world would she say that?

She talked to us about what it took to be married and even pulled out her Bible to read us scripture. She read to us Ephesians 5: 22-24:

"Wives, submit to your husbands as to the Lord. For the husband is the head of the wife as Christ is the head of the Church, his body, of which he is the Savior. Now as the Church

submits to Christ, so also wives should submit to their husbands."

Victor's eyes quickly shifted to me and although he wasn't fond of my religion, he knew a little bit about it.

Then, my mother read from Genesis 2:24:

" . . . And a man will leave his mother and join his wife and the two will become one flesh . . . ."

She continued to explain to Victor that the man was the head of the household and the wife was subservient to him. I saw Victor's ears perk up when he heard that. Although my mother only read a portion of the scripture, it reinforced Victor's right to do whatever he wanted to me. He seemed amused as he listened to my mother while he shook his head in agreement. She talked to us for about an hour, while I got fidgety and just wanted it to be over. Deep in my heart, I knew she meant well, but she did not know Victor the way I did. Saying things like that to him just boosted his ego and made my situation worse. The last thing Victor needed was to hear that I needed to be subservient to him. As Victor left my house, he kissed me goodbye and told me he would talk to me when he arrived in Georgia. I knew he had a smile on his face all the way to his mother's house thinking of all the malicious things he had permission to do to me.

Chapter 6

Winter 1985 — Preparing For Life On Fort Bragg

My parents eventually adjusted to the fact that I was a married woman and pretty much didn't say anymore to me about eloping with Victor. Granted, I didn't have my dream wedding, but I was married nonetheless. Victor's Permanent Duty Station would be at Ft. Bragg in North Carolina and I couldn't come down there until he got a car and found an apartment. The plan was that after I moved down there, we would live off-base until a house on-base became available. He also told me he wasn't coming up for the holidays because he was trying to save money too. I began to think that maybe he was finally settling into being a responsible married man and things would change for the better. Although it wasn't any fun spending my holidays without my husband, I didn't complain. I just thought of it as one of those sacrifices I had to make as his wife. I knew he would come up whenever he could to see me and we would spend a few hours together before he went back to North Carolina. Years later, I found out that although Victor did come to see me, there were many times he came to New York and didn't tell me. I didn't know if he did that to spy on me or if he had another girlfriend in New York.

We were married for about five months when I decided to go to North Carolina to see Victor. I was excited because it would be the first time I traveled alone out of state. He lived in the barracks on Fort Bragg and was on track to being promoted to the rank of Sergeant, which at twenty-one years old, was a great accomplishment. When I got off the bus in North Carolina, he told me we could stay with his Army friend Harry* and his wife Tracey.*

"We're going straight to Harry and Tracey's house," he said.

I was excited to meet his friends and felt like we were finally doing "couple" things. We arrived at Harry and Tracey's house and when they hugged me, I got the feeling they were good people. Harry and Tracey were both from St. Louis, Missouri and Tracey spoke with a deep southern accent. Although Harry was in the military, they didn't live on the base. Rather, they lived in Fayetteville, about twenty minutes from the base.

"Nice to finally meet you Ivette," Tracey and Harry said.

After setting us up in their extra bedroom, Tracey offered to drive me around and show me Fayetteville. I quickly unpacked, got in the car with Tracey and left Victor in the house with Harry. As we drove around, she gave me the grand tour of Fayetteville. Tracey asked me a lot of questions, including what it was like to live in New York and that one day she wanted to visit. She showed me where the malls were, the nice restaurants and a quick way to get to Fort Bragg. We were out for about an hour when Tracey realized she needed to get home to cook dinner and I gladly agreed to help her. When we got back to her house to start dinner, Victor and Harry were still in the living room talking about work. Shortly after dinner, I couldn't eat another bite of food because I felt nauseous, so I went to the bathroom to vomit. I came out of the bathroom looking so bad that Tracey offered to take me to Womack Army Medical Center, the hospital on base, while Victor and Harry stayed at home with their infant son.

When we got there and spoke to the intake nurse, she instructed us to go to the waiting room. When I was called into the doctor's office, I told him what my symptoms were, that I had a fever, was feeling very nauseous and couldn't keep my food down. After asking me the standard perfunctory questions, he examined me.

"You have honeymooner's disease," he said.

"What is that?" I asked.

"In other words, you have pelvic inflammatory disease."

I became upset because I didn't know anything about this type of disease.

"How did I get it?" I asked the doctor.

"Oh it just happens sometimes from too much sexual activity. Nothing to worry about," he replied.

In reality, I learned later that pelvic inflammatory disease (PID) is a term that refers to an infection of the uterus. It is a common and serious complication of some sexually transmitted infections (STIs), especially chlamydia and gonorrhea. Also, a person whose partner has more than one sex partner is at greater risk of developing PID because of the potential for more exposure to infectious agents.

The doctor wrote a prescription for me for an antibiotic and told me that Victor and I would have to take it and that I would eventually be okay.

I left the doctor's office and went back into the emergency room waiting area where Tracey waited for me.

"Is everything okay?" she asked me.

"Yeah, the doctor told me I had PID."

"Oh," was all she said.

On the way back to the house, I said very little except thanking her for taking me to the hospital.

"Gurl, that's okay," Tracey said.

We were quiet for a few minutes before she spoke again.

"You know gurl, you don't know me from Adam, but I feel like I gotta tell you something, 'cause if it was me, I'd want somebody to tell me. I know that Victor's your husband and you're gonna believe him, but…"

"Tell me what?" I asked.

"You have PID because Victor gave it to you."

"What?" I replied.

I was shocked that she could say that to me considering we just met.

She continued, "You don't get PID from having too much sex; you got it because Victor was screwin' around and not using protection."

I couldn't believe what I was hearing, and it annoyed me. I knew I wasn't cheating on Victor but was naïve to think that I couldn't have gotten it from him.

"But Victor said he would never cheat on me," I told her.

"He's gonna tell you that and he's gonna keep tellin' you that. I'm not sayin' this 'cause I wanna make trouble between you and your husband. I don't particularly care for Victor and he knows it. Besides, he also knows I'm not afraid of him. I actually seen Victor wit' other women."

I couldn't argue with that because she saw more than I did! I still wasn't sure how to take the news that Tracey just gave me, so I kept my mouth shut. Meanwhile, my mind ran a mile a minute. On one hand, she actually saw Victor with other women; I, on the other hand, only knew what he told me. But why would he marry me if he wasn't going to be faithful? Then my mind went back to the question I had some months earlier but didn't pay any attention to — why did Victor have a sudden change of heart at the last minute and decide to marry me?

We finally arrived at her house and she parked the car in the driveway. When we got inside, Victor asked me how everything went.

"I'm fine," I said, because I didn't want to discuss anything in front of Harry and Tracey.

"I'm still feeling queasy, so I'm going to bed," I told him as he followed me into the bedroom.

Once we were behind closed doors, I calmly told him what the doctor told me. When I told him about the antibiotics the doctor gave me and that he would have to take them too, he exploded.

"What the fuck are you talking about? You've been cheating on me, haven't you? You fucked around on me and gave me something?"

What the hell was wrong with him? Why was he blaming me? If I was the one cheating and the one that gave him something, why would I tell him? That's when I started to believe what Tracey told me. Victor blaming me was a dead giveaway that he was being unfaithful. Besides, I also knew that Victor had a habit of shifting blame back on me because he had done it so many times before.

As these thoughts ran through my head, I started to cry.

I didn't mention to Victor that Tracey told me she saw him with other women. He kept insulting me and accusing me of cheating on him, calling me names and, through my tears, I denied it all.

"No, I haven't cheated on you!"

"I told you if you EVER cheated on me, I would kill you!" he said through clenched teeth as he charged at me and put his hands around my throat. I struggled with him and tried not to scream as the walls in Harry and Tracey's house were so thin.

"I told you, I wasn't cheating on you! Don't try to blame this on me because YOU were the one cheating on me!" As he was choking me, he spoke to me through clenched teeth.

"Don't tell me what the fuck I'm doing!" he said as we fell on the bed and he pressed his knees on my chest.

I struggled with him to let me go. In my mind, I couldn't believe this was happening! He finally got off of me and just before he walked out of the room, his demeanor quickly changed to look as if nothing was wrong. Trying to stifle my tears, I took off my clothes, put on my pajamas, took the medication and tried to go to sleep. The more I thought about it, the more I believed Tracey. I realized the next day when I looked in the prescription bottle and counted the pills, that Victor never took any of the medication.

My trip to North Carolina definitely wasn't the trip that I'd hoped it would be — a newly married couple enjoying each other's company and having fun. Instead, it turned into a nightmare, with my getting sick and finding out that Victor cheated on me. I used to dream that once Victor and I got married, we would travel around the world and enjoy being married. That was very different from what was really happening.

Victor was quiet as he drove me back to the bus station. When we got there and I got out the car, he didn't get out to kiss me goodbye. As soon as I closed the car door, he sped off.

On the bus ride back to New York, I thought about the weekend's events and it depressed me. I thought more and more about Victor attacking me and the fact that not only had he cheated on me, but that he gave me a disease. When finally I got back to my mother's house, I acted as if nothing happened over the weekend with Victor. I didn't know what to do, because I took my marriage vows seriously and getting a divorce wasn't an option. Victor went back to calling me collect as usual and not offering to send me money towards the phone bill, just like he did before. When he called, he didn't mention anything about what happened over the weekend or the fact that he cheated on me.

As far as the collect calls were concerned, I felt I didn't have the right to not accept the calls from my husband, although it wasn't right that he didn't offer me money for my mother's bill. Nonetheless, I didn't complain or ask him for money. I just gave my mother money out of my paycheck for the bill when it came, becoming frustrated with spending my money while Victor kept his and spent it on what he wanted to spend it on. Feeling the pinch and believing that Victor was financially abusing me, I told him he had to send me some money for the collect calls.

"What are you talking about? Why are you asking me for money again? What? Did you marry me for my money?"

It wasn't the first time Victor accused me of marrying him for his money, as if I was some poor little girl looking to marry a rich man. Victor rich? Not in his wildest dreams!

"If you're going to continue to call my parent's house collect, then it's only right you send me money to pay the phone bill," I chimed in.

"Well then let me get off the phone," and Victor hung up.

I was getting tired of Victor's games, so I called him back. This time, I got another officer on the phone who conveniently told me that Victor wasn't at his desk. I don't know how Victor could have gotten away from his desk so quickly, but figured he was dodging me and had someone tell me that he wasn't there. This officer happened to be Victor's commanding officer, Staff Sergeant Jackson.* He was cordial towards me and congratulated me on getting married, but I didn't see anything to be happy about.

"You know, I want to tell you a few things, kind of like an orientation. I couldn't help but overhear you and Victor's conversation. Did you know that once you are married to an active duty member and you don't live together, that the military gives the active duty member extra money to send to the family? It's called Basic Allowance for Quarters." I was speechless.

"No, I didn't know that, but we don't have any children yet," I told him.

"It doesn't matter. You're married. Let me see, Victor's rank is Specialist Fourth Grade, so he should be sending you about $250 per month."

"He hasn't sent me a dime," I told him. I could hear Staff Sergeant Jackson take a deep breath.

"I'll make sure to speak to Victor about this, especially since he's been getting this money since you two were married. Well Ivette it was nice talking to you. I look forward to meeting you when you come down here."

I said goodbye, then he hung up. I always wondered where Victor got extra money to buy his car; now I know.

I called Victor the next day and confronted him with this latest development. I wanted him to know that I knew what he was doing.

"Victor, I was told that you're supposed to be sending me money as a result of being married and we've been married for about six months. So, at $250 per month, that comes to $1,500. Some of that money could have been sent to me to pay for your collect calls. What have you been doing with the money?"

I wanted to see if he was going to tell me the truth. As usual, he didn't answer the question. Instead, he shifted the blame and replied with more accusations.

"Who the fuck are you to be questioning me? That's my money to do what the fuck I want to do with it!" he responded.

I sat quietly and listened to him as he created this scenario where all of a sudden, he was the victim.

"I can't help but get the feeling you married me for my money," he said. He was about to continue when I cut him off.

"What money? I didn't even know about this until Sergeant Jackson told me yesterday!"

"Well, I just bought myself a new car. I don't have to send the money to you," he said.

It was no surprise that he would say that to me.

"Who married who for money? Oh, now I get it. You married me so you can get extra money, only instead of sending it to me, you're keeping it for yourself to buy yourself a car, while I'm paying for your collect calls out of my paycheck! So, who married who for what?" I asked him.

If this is what being married was supposed to be like, it's REALLY overrated. We were both quiet for what seemed like minutes. Then I hung up on him. I didn't know much about the military, but I was sure about to get a crash course in how things are done on Fort Bragg. I quickly realized that I couldn't trust anything Victor said or did and if I want to know the truth, I would have to find things out for myself.

Chapter 7

Summer 1986 — Maybe He'll Change

Since it was clear that I couldn't rely on Victor and wasn't sure if I could find a job when I got to North Carolina, I made sure to save as much money as I could. Deep inside, I knew that Victor wasn't doing right by me because if a man loves a woman, he would treat her with love and kindness. So much was wrong with my relationship with Victor, but I really wanted to give my marriage a chance.

I didn't care to speak to Susan much after we got married, yet, I always had an uncomfortable feeling that she knew something I didn't. On several occasions, she would call just to chat, as if she was trying to get information from me so she could tell Victor. I didn't think Susan had a sincere bone in her body and that made me suspicious of her.

I always wondered if I made the right choice in marrying Victor. When he called off the wedding before, the thought crossed my mind that maybe God was telling me that he wasn't the one for me. When my inner voice spoke to me, I ignored it and instead, made excuses for Victor. A small part of me felt that he would change once I moved down to North Carolina. Maybe the strain of a long-distance marriage was taking its toll on him.

Because he wasn't paying for the collect calls he made to me, I limited his calls to ten minutes. He still received money from the military and wasn't sending it to me. I wasn't going to concern myself with the money, although I was entitled to it and it could have helped me while I lived in New York.

Our first wedding anniversary was right around the corner when

Victor found a furnished apartment at Cambridge Arms in Fayetteville that would be ready soon. I was excited, as I had prepared for a whole year to finally begin my life with my husband. It wasn't easy being married and living apart and even though I found out he cheated on me, I silently forgave him and tried not to let it occupy my thoughts. To prepare for my move, I bought items that I wanted for the apartment and packed them away in my mother's house. Victor was due to come to New York to pick me up and all my energy was focused on being completely packed by the time he got there. I was in my room gathering my clothes when my mother came in.

"You know, I wish you would really reconsider moving down to North Carolina. Why don't you just stay up here and work until Victor gets out of the Army?"

It wasn't the first time she said that to me. When I talked to my mother, I needed to choose my words carefully. I wanted her to know that I was grown and was willing to accept responsibility for my actions, regardless of whether others thought they were right or wrong.

"What kind of marriage would that be Ma? I know you didn't approve of Victor and me getting married and I know you didn't like it when we eloped, but I have to give my marriage a chance. If things don't work out, then I'll know I gave it my best shot."

My mom stood there and looked at me. I wasn't sure what that look meant but she knew she couldn't argue with what I just told her.

Victor finally arrived at my mother's house to get me and we had two days to get back to Fort Bragg. Our neighbor across the hall, an elderly couple who raised pure-bred Siamese cats, knew I was moving so they gave me a Siamese kitten as a going away present. After Victor and I spent time going back and forth from my mom's house to the car, the car was finally packed up. I hugged my dad and kissed my mom goodbye, feeling sad that I was leaving home, my family and friends. I had mixed feelings about doing this but felt things would be okay once I got in the car with Victor and started our trip to North Carolina.

As we drove to North Carolina, my head was filled with dreams of starting a new life in another state as well as my hopes that things between us would change for the better.

We finally got to North Carolina in just seven hours, around 3 a.m. The management office for the complex we were moving into didn't open until 9 a.m., so Victor and I checked into a hotel with my new kitten to get a few hours sleep. A few hours later, we checked out of the hotel and went to the management office to sign the lease for the apartment. Once we arrived at Cambridge Arms Apartments, located on All American Highway, Victor pulled the car in front of the management office and told me to stay in the car. While I waited, I noticed the complex was maintained decently with lots of grass and it was conveniently next to the highway. Directly across the road were Bennigans, Shoney's and some other restaurants. The mall was within walking distance and the supermarket was close as well.

Although I felt I should be inside the office with Victor to sign the lease, I tried to be the humble and subservient wife by obeying my husband and allowing him to take care of business without interference from me. I had no reason to think that after driving to New York to get me, then driving back to North Carolina that my own husband would try to throw me out. But, against my better judgment, I waited patiently in the car while Victor went inside to take care of everything. Victor eventually came back to the car with the lease and keys to our new apartment.

While he turned the car around, I looked at the lease and mentioned out loud that maybe I should have signed the lease too.

"You didn't need to sign the lease. It's my apartment, not yours," Victor said.

I felt my ears getting hot, as they usually did when I got angry, but didn't say a word. It was already going to be a long day, moving all my stuff into the apartment and Victor still had to go back to the barracks and get his things. When we arrived at the new apartment, Victor helped me move my things inside. I was about to go with him so I could help move his things from the barracks when told me to stay at the apartment.

I didn't think much of him telling me to stay there, so I busied myself in the apartment, cleaning and unpacking while Victor was away. It was a decently furnished one bedroom apartment on the first floor, with a well-worn sofa and loveseat with a floral print on it that looked like someone threw up on it, army green wood paneling on the walls and brown carpeting on the floor. The galley-styled kitchen was small and narrow with minimum counter space, a refrigerator and electric stove. The electric stove was something new to me because we always had a gas stove at home. The large bedroom had a full-sized bed and dresser and had the same color carpeting and army green wood paneling as the living room. The rent was reasonable at only $250 per month. Victor eventually got back home from the barracks with the first car load of his things and had to make a second trip back to the barracks. While he was away, I saw some mail that Victor dumped on the table before he left. In the pile was a letter addressed to him from someone named Lisa.* It was in plain sight, so I picked up the letter and read it. It turned out to be a love letter from her to Victor. She told him how much she loved him and how she didn't want to leave him, but she got stationed somewhere else in the Army and was upset that they couldn't get married. I couldn't believe what I was reading! The letter was dated just a few months before I moved to North Carolina! How dare Victor do this to me again? I decided that I was going to get even — I was going to let this woman know that Victor was married, since it looks like he didn't tell her himself. I wrote a letter on a piece of toilet tissue and told her that he was married and to stay away from him. I thought the toilet tissue was a nice touch because I didn't want to waste a good sheet of paper on this bitch. I put the "letter" into an envelope with the intention on mailing it to Lisa the next day and hid it in my dresser drawer. Victor finally came home with what I thought was the last of his belongings, so I decided to confront him with this latest development. I didn't tell him about the letter I wrote.

"Who's Lisa?" I asked him.

"None of your damn business! This is my motherfuckin' house and you don't go through my things! I should put your ass out!" he screamed at me.

Here we go with the "it's my house" speech!

"I'm going back to the barracks." He stormed out and slammed the door.

I knew he wasn't going to answer my questions about Lisa, so my mind turned to other pressing matters. My mind went back to when I stayed in the car while Victor went in and took care of the lease at the management office. My inside voice told me to go to the management office and sign the lease so he couldn't throw me out when the mood struck him. Once the car disappeared from the parking lot, I walked over to the office and asked the manager if I could sign the original lease for our apartment, since we only had a copy.

"Sure, no problem." the manager asked.

I didn't want him to think anything was amiss, so I said to him with a smile on my face, "I wasn't around when my husband signed the lease, so I want to add my name to it as well."

"Oh, okay," he said.

I showed him my military ID, then he went into a file cabinet and pulled out the lease. I examined it carefully.

"So, when I add my name to the lease, can he still throw me out?" I asked the Manager.

The manager had a puzzled look on his face.

"No, he can't throw you out as long as your name is on the lease," he said to me as I signed my name where it said "Co-tenant."

He also told me that the original lease in the management office was the only one that mattered. I thanked the manager and walked back to our apartment and didn't bother to get a copy of the new lease.

Victor came home shortly after that. As I put my things away in the dresser, he started in on me again.

"Who the fuck do you think you are? I should throw you out this house for fuckin' with me!"

Hmmm, twice within a couple of hours he threatens to throw me out! I had a feeling Victor would pull a stunt like that, so I told him with all the confidence I could muster,

"It's not YOUR house, it's OUR house!" He looked at me, shocked because it didn't register right away with him what I had done.

"It's MY house, because my name is only one on the lease!" he screamed.

I smiled on the inside before I replied to him.

"Not anymore!" I told him, with a matter-of-fact tone in my voice.

The look on his face was priceless as he tried to figure out what I did. His face changed when he put it all together.

"You BITCH! I can't believe you went behind my back and did that shit!" he screamed as he charged towards where I was standing by the front door. He flung the door open and tried to push me out of the apartment into the night.

"This is my goddamned house!" he screamed as he shoved me out the door.

This was my first night in my apartment with my husband and already he was trying to throw me out! We struggled as he tried to push me out and I fought to stay in. I fought him with everything I had although, at 6 feet and approximately 180 pounds he was much bigger than me and I was at only 125 pounds. We struggled, sweating and panting until we ended up in the back lawn behind our apartment where we both eventually fell on the ground. Then he straddled me and started choking me. I broke his grip and with all my strength, flipped him over and stuffed grass in his mouth and screamed at him.

"You're not throwing ME out you fuckin' bastard!"

I didn't care if anyone heard me or called the police. After about an hour of fighting, I finally got off of him, dirty and covered with grass and went back into the apartment and slammed the door. I called his mother, crying and screaming to the top of my lungs.

"If you love your son, you'll tell him to keep his fuckin' hands to himself!"

Susan knew I was pissed because she never heard me curse like that before. She asked me what happened and I told her. Victor came into the apartment minutes later and snatched the phone away from me, then walked into the bedroom and slammed the door. After a few minutes and some laughing, he threw the phone back at me. Susan tried to sound as if she really wanted to help me, but I knew better.

"Do you want to come home? Because if you do, I'll have a ticket at the airport waiting for you." I couldn't believe the nerve of her!

"What's that going to solve? I just got here! How is a plane ticket going to make him stop hitting me?" I said to her.

What was wrong with that woman? How did she think I was going to get to the airport? Click my heels? She got quiet and I finally realized that talking to Susan about her son was a dead issue. After I got off the phone with her, I said nothing more to Victor. I took a shower, changed into my pajamas and plopped on the couch. I eventually fell asleep, knowing that in the morning, I was going ahead with my plan to mail my letter to Lisa.

I knew when I mailed the letter to Lisa, it would only be a matter of days before she called Victor and told him what I did. When he found out, he was furious.

"Who the fuck do you think you are sending a letter to my friend?" he screamed.

"Well, it seems that you forgot to tell her you were married. But then, the only reason you married me was because you couldn't marry her!" I yelled back.

Then Victor became indignant.

"I told you to stay the fuck out of my things! I'm the man of this house! Anything I do outside this house is none of your business! My friend was pissed that you did that!"

Pissed? Why is he telling me how "pissed" his friend is? I'm the one who moved to North Carolina to be with him, only to find out that he wanted to marry someone else! So that's why Victor called off the wedding, only to want to elope months later! I also wondered if Susan knew anything about this. To think that Victor married me as a consolation prize because he couldn't be with the one he wanted really hurt.

As Victor stormed out of the apartment, I plopped down on the couch. I was lonely and homesick, so I called my family back in New York. I didn't allude to what had happened when I first got down there or that Victor was still hitting me. Just talking on the phone with my family was enough to make me feel better.

A few days passed before I decided to look for a job. Since I had no means of transportation because Victor used the car to drive to work, I had to walk up and down McPherson Church Road to look for a job.

Victor came home from work one day and yelled at me as he walked in the door.

"Who the fuck do you think I am? You think I'm made out of money?"

He shook the phone bill at me, pointing out all the long-distance calls to my family. I thought, here we go again about marrying him for his money.

"How am I supposed to pay this?" he said.

Mind you, the bill was all of $40.

"With the money you have been collecting from the military for being married to me," I said.

I wanted to tell him we were even because he didn't send me money for all the collect calls, but changed my mind and thought better of it.

Next thing, SLAP! Right across my face. Then he moved closer to me.

"Who the fuck are you, talking to me like that! I should throw your ass out. All you do is sit on your ass, eat my food and run up my bills. You ain't got no job, nothin'. Know what, you can't call home anymore unless you ask me for permission." I was still rubbing my face from where he slapped me.

"But you call YOUR mother!" I said to him through my tears.

"It's my fuckin' house and my fuckin' phone and I do what the fuck I want!" Victor said.

I tried to walk away from him, but he grabbed my arm and snatched me back.

"I'll know if you've been on the phone making long-distance calls. You'd better find a job and quick!"

I resented him for trying to make me feel like a freeloader or as if I were taking advantage of him. I tried to tell Victor that I gave up my job to be with him and that it was hard finding a job in Fayetteville without a car.

"Then you'd better start walking," he said.

He ran off the names of different restaurants near where we lived.

"There's Bennigans, Shoney's and Burger King down the road. You should be able to find a job there."

He tried to make it seem like I was some lazy woman looking for some man to take care of her and I resented that. As his wife, I knew that I was supposed to pull my weight, but he treated me differently than that. While other young people my age got jobs in McDonalds and Burger King, I had only had experience working in an office environment.

Later that night, after all the hurtful things he said to me earlier, Victor still expected me to fulfill my "wifely" duties. How was I supposed to feel like having sex with him when he made it a daily sport to make me feel like shit? I really didn't feel like it and he didn't care about what I wanted, as long as he got his. When he was done, he rolled over and went to sleep. I got up and went into the bathroom to wash off, then into the living room to watch TV until I drifted off to sleep. I had to get up in a few hours to find a job.

The next morning after Victor left for work, I put on my best interview clothes, walked along McPherson Church Road and made a right on the All American Highway to where Cross County Mall was located. I thought that between my high school diploma and work experience I would be able to find a decent job, but I was sadly mistaken. I spent the next two weeks getting up every morning, walking alongside the road and going to different places to look for a job because Victor still wouldn't let me use the car. I was determined to find work because I knew that if I was going to have anything, it wasn't going to come from Victor — I had to get it myself. At the time, it didn't bother me that Victor wouldn't let me use the car, although I could have dropped him off at work, gone job hunting, then picked him up after work. Since I knew I wasn't married to that kind of person, I got up every day and did what I had to do. After weeks of looking, I couldn't find a job anywhere because I was either overqualified, underqualified or didn't have a college degree. One day I talked to Tracey about my problems finding a job.

"Gurl, 'bout the only place you can get a job down here is by either working on post or at a fast-food restaurant," Tracey said.

"Geez! Well maybe I could go to college down here and take a few classes. Maybe I can get a better job that way," I said to her.

"Gurl, I get so mad at Victor that he don't tell you nothin' 'bout what you entitled to," she said.

"What are you talking about?" I asked. She took a deep breath as she shook her head in disgust.

"As his wife, you are entitled to a lot of things. You could take college classes for seven dollars a credit."

"Oh shoot! It would be good if I could do that. I'm going to talk to Victor tonight about it."

I thought it would be a good idea to go to college and find a decent job before I had children.

When Victor came home from work, he dropped his things on the floor and sat on the couch. I decided that was the best time to approach him.

"You know, since it seems so hard for me to find a good job down here without a college degree, I thought I could take some courses on base so I can get a better job. I found out that it only costs seven dollars a credit."

Victor looked at me as if I were crazy.

"Really? Now, how are you going to get to school?" he asked.

What a dumb question! I told him that I could ride to the base with him in the morning and he could pick me up after work. I wanted to make sure I had all my bases covered so he wouldn't say no.

"You don't have a job. Who's going to pay for you to go to school?" he said.

I told him he could pay for me to go to school and I would reimburse him when I got a job. I knew that Victor was taking correspondence courses to build up college credits to get his next rank, so I thought he would understand what I was trying to do.

"You must be outta your fuckin' mind! Once again, you ain't got no job. Who's going to pay for the extra gas I use to take you to school and pick you up? What if the car breaks down from driving you around — do you have money to fix the car?"

I could feel the tears welling up in my eyes. I never really understood how someone could be so selfish.

"What's so bad about going to school if I can get a good job so I can pull my weight around here? Why are you opposed to me going to school? You're not the only one around here who wants to better themselves."

Victor just shrugged his shoulders.

"Cause my money is my money and I ain't going to spend it on you. You were living in a rat trap when I met you. I took you out of the gutter, married you and turned you into somebody! You should be grateful for that!"

As usual, I couldn't believe what I was hearing. Talking to me as if he was better than me! At that moment, I looked around the apartment, with the army green paneling on the walls, cheap furniture and carpeting on the floor.

"If this is what it's like to be somebody, you should have left me in the gutter," I spat back.

Victor just laughed and continued watching TV.

"Well then, I'm going to the doctor tomorrow to get birth control, because I'm not ready to start having kids yet," I said to Victor.

I didn't want to just work and be at home and have children. I wanted to better myself but Victor wouldn't hear of it. He seemed annoyed that I was interrupting his show. His mood changed when I talked about getting birth control.

"Why would you want to put that poison in your body?" he said.

"I just don't want to have any kids right now," I replied.

I realized that I wasn't going to have the storybook life with Victor. I could at least do something for myself while I was still young, but Victor sabotaged any attempt I made to independent.

"I'm concerned about your health because that stuff isn't safe for you to take," he said.

Victor all of a sudden tried to make it seem as if he cared about me. It was like he was Jekyll and Hyde; nice one second and mean the next.

"Well, I'd like for a doctor to tell me that," I spat back.

I was tired of him acting as if he knew what was better for me than I did.

Victor stood up and pointed his finger in my face.

"See, that's what pisses me off about you. You don't listen. That's why I end up slapping the shit out of you. You're hardheaded! I don't want you puttin' that shit in your body. Besides, as long as you're barefoot and pregnant, I'll always know where you are."

When he said that, it just made me angrier. How dare he talk to me as if he were my father? We argued back and forth for a while until I just gave up and went into the bedroom to lie down. As I lay in bed, my mind went back to my religious teachings where I had to "obey" my husband and "respect" his authority. A small part of me felt that he cared because he didn't want me to "put that shit in my body." I did know that women could have problems conceiving after being on birth control for long periods of time. Maybe he was right about that. But then, my choice to go on birth control should be my decision, not his. I wanted to have children when I wanted to, not when he said I could! What was I going to do? I felt I was lying around with a target on my back waiting to get pregnant. When we first met, I thought Victor would have been a good father and I always wanted kids, but now, I knew I didn't want to have any children with him — especially since he was abusive. On the other hand, he was my husband and I wouldn't be a good Christian wife if I refused to have children, no matter how badly my husband treated me. Abortion was against my religion but I never heard anything in the Kingdom Hall about birth control. Would I be going against God's will to be on birth control?

Chapter 8

Fall 1986 — Falling Apart

Each day passed with Victor becoming more and more verbally abusive towards me. He would go to work during the week and on the weekend, would spend all day out of the house. His favorite excuses were "I'm going to play ball with the guys today," or, "I got called in for duty today." The only explanation I could come up with was that Victor was seeing someone. On Fridays, he worked as a disc jockey in the Non-Commissioned Officer's Club on base and never asked me if I wanted to go with him; he would just pack up his records and leave. I was lonely and felt depressed when he left, wondering why my own husband didn't want to spend time with me. Victor did everything he could to keep me isolated from my family and friends and it eventually affected my sleeping and eating habits. I felt as if Victor had a leash around my neck and he was pulling it tighter. Ever since Victor got mad at me for calling my family, he wanted to make me afraid to use the phone by playing mind games. He would leave the house for a few minutes, then come back and press redial on the phone to see if I had called anyone. Victor wanted to control everything I did, including where I went and wouldn't even allow me to use the car so I could go to school. To make matters worse, I was too proud to pack my things and move back to New York.

Although Tracey occasionally stopped by to keep me company, she wasn't a replacement for my husband. But, she was the only person Victor couldn't scare away because she didn't like him and knew what he was up to. I talked to Tracey one time about how Victor abused me.

She was the only person that really knew what was going on.

"Gurl, you better call his commanding officer and tell him what Victor is doing to you. I bet he'll stop then."

At twenty-one years of age, Victor was on his way to becoming one of the youngest Sergeants in the Army and was being watched closely by his superiors. So, I never called the police when Victor hit me because I didn't want to cause trouble for him. Being in the military and rising through the ranks fed Victor's ego and his twisted need for power and control. Victor used to tell me the military had a saying, "If you can't control your family, you can't control your troops."

Besides, I was raised with the belief that whatever happened in your home, stayed in your home. Although I felt awkward talking to Tracey about my problems with Victor, it made me feel better when I was able to get some of the pain I felt off my chest. I knew Tracey wasn't giving me advice to cause trouble. She was a military wife too and simply told me things she felt I should know.

A few days later I confronted Victor about being in the house all alone on the weekends.

"What did I do to you to make you treat me like this?" I asked him.

"What do you mean?" he replied.

"You leave me in the house all weekend with no transportation. Do you think I'm stupid? I know you're seeing someone," I responded.

Victor never liked being challenged and always had to have the final say. I saw the fire in his eyes when he ran up to me, slapped me then pushed me down on the couch.

"Look! I told you before, that's none of your fucking business! What I do outside of this house don't have nothin' to do with you!"

I was tired of Victor pushing me around and tired of being hit for no reason, as if I were the dog he would come home and kick. I finally got up and walked towards the kitchen with tears in my eyes, thinking about the advice Tracey gave me.

"That's it! I'm tired of you putting your hands on me! Put your hands on me one more time and I'm making a call to your commanding officer!"

Victor's whole demeanor changed for the worse in a snap. He ran towards me, put me in a headlock and tried to ram my head into the wall. But just as quickly, I twisted my body so that I went into the back cushions of the couch instead. He pushed me down on the couch, straddled me and then choked me with fire in his eyes.

"How dare you threaten my career? You fuckin' bitch! You ain't nobody! You ain't shit! I'll kill you if you EVER call my commanding officer and make me look bad!"

I cried and screamed for him to get off me, but I couldn't because his hands were so tight around my throat. Then, all of a sudden, his grip slowly loosened. God, I must be crazy because I could have sworn that when I started to cry, his grip loosened, but when I stopped crying and started fighting him back, that's when he tightened his grip.

"I will fuck you up!" He slapped me until I started crying again.

Once he was satisfied I was still crying, he got up, walked towards the bedroom and slammed the door. I couldn't take it anymore. I couldn't understand why he felt he could treat me like this, then perceive me as a threat to his career because I wanted him to stop hitting me. It was as if he felt he could abuse me without assuming responsibility for his actions. The days I spent by myself in the house were filled with loneliness. I couldn't figure out why he didn't want to spend time with me and it caused me to cry constantly. I couldn't tell my family because they would judge me and say "I told you so." I was so depressed that I wanted all the pain of the physical and verbal abuse to go away. I began to think that being dead was a far cry better than what I was feeling.

It was Friday and Victor prepared to go out to the club. While he was in the bedroom getting dressed, he sang out loud to himself and soon the smell of his cologne wafted into the living room where I sat. He acted as if nothing happened, as if he didn't just strangle me. I was at my wits end since I had only been in North Carolina a couple of months and nothing was going the way I had hoped. All I could think about was a way to end the pain.

Victor had a prescription for Parafon Forte, a powerful muscle relaxant that he received from his dentist on base months before for oral surgery. I was familiar with it since I had taken it for pain from a car accident when I was fifteen. I figured if I took the pills, I would look like I was sleeping on the couch and Victor would walk past me right out of the house. So I took ten pills, pushed the prescription bottle deep under the couch, turned on the TV and laid down on the sofa. I knew what the medication would do to me; soon the muscle relaxants would kick in, then I would drift off into a relaxing and peaceful sleep, then my heart would just stop. At that time, having peace in my life for a change — peace of mind, body and spirit appealed to me even if it meant dying. I don't know how much time passed before I succumbed to the effect of the pills. My body became so relaxed that I couldn't keep my eyes open or lift my arms. I felt euphoric as a result of the drugs and I didn't feel any pain. As the sound of the TV slowly faded, I heard Victor's voice.

"See ya!" he said as he walked towards the door. I heard him but couldn't move.

"I said see ya!" he said again.

I felt him shaking me but couldn't respond. He kept calling my name.

"Ivette!"

By then, the pills had already started to take effect. I remembered being lifted up and hit in the face by cold air. Then I heard various sounds — a siren, people talking and cars. Then the smell of ammonia overtook my senses. I opened my eyes a little to see that I was on a bed in a brightly lit room. I heard someone asking me my name, what I took, how old I was and it all sounded like a whisper.

I just wanted to be left alone to go to sleep. Then the smell of ammonia hit me again. I was getting annoyed because these people would not leave me alone.

"Can you hear me Ivette?" I had trouble moving my mouth, so I just nodded my head.

"We're going to pump your stomach, but you have to help us by inserting this tube down your throat. Then we're going to pour nitrate and charcoal down the tube into your stomach to make you throw up. How many pills did you take?" I still had trouble opening my mouth and holding my head up.

"Five? Ten?"

I nodded my head when he got to ten. Someone put my hands around a large plastic tube and helped me guide it down my throat. I could feel my stomach filling up with a strange, bubbly liquid that burned. As I threw up, the doctor counted the pills.

"Okay, I see three. Okay, I see four more."

As time went by, the effects of the pills started to wear off and I was able to put faces to the voices I heard.

"You gave us quite a scare, Ivette," the doctor said.

For a few seconds, I thought I died and went to heaven. That was, until I saw Victor standing behind the doctor. The it quickly dawned on me that I was alive and in an emergency room.

"SHIT! Why couldn't Victor just leave me alone?" I thought to myself. The doctor continued talking.

"Your husband tells me that you two had a spat." It took a few seconds for it to register in my mind what the doctor just said. I shook my head.

"That's not true. He's been abusing me for quite a while."

Victor cut me off in mid-sentence and spoke to me in a condescending manner, as if he was afraid I would say too much and reveal the truth.

"Now Ivette, every time we have an argument, you think the world is coming to an end. Doctor, I love my wife. I don't know why she would do something like this. I've never laid a hand on her. We started to argue and I pushed her down on the couch. Then she went and took all those pills."

I stared at the both of them. I could tell by the look on the doctor's face that he believed everything Victor said. And, I could tell by the look on Victor's face that he got the doctor to believe him. I hated the way Victor manipulated every situation to shift the blame away from himself and on to me. This was one of several times I've heard Victor lie to save his own skin, even if it made me look weak and mentally fragile. I decided not to say much after that because after having my stomach pumped, I wasn't in the mood to play Victor's game.

When Victor pulled the doctor away from my bed to the opposite side of the room out of my earshot, I saw his hands become animated while the doctor nodded his head. As I watched Victor, I realized that he must be telling the doctor another grandiose story to make me look crazy, which explained why the doctor never believed me. When I look back at that experience, it became clear to me that doctors, police and legal system weren't trained to recognize the signs of domestic violence and abuse or even believe the victim.

When the doctor walked over to my bed, he told me he was going to keep me in the hospital for a few nights for observation in their psychiatric ward. I shook my head as my mind was still foggy from the pills and I wasn't in the mood to argue.

Just before the doctor left my bed, Victor came over and patted me on the hand as if he was really concerned about me.

"I'm leaving now. Don't worry honey, I'll be back tomorrow with some clothes for you."

The next day, still groggy from the night before, my sore throat reminded me of my suicide attempt and my stomach being pumped. As I got out of the bed, I noticed a young woman who shared the room with me, sitting on her bed with clothes on that looked very familiar. Then it dawned on me that she had on my clothes! Cautious as to how to approach her because I didn't know how she would react, I asked for my clothes back.

"Excuse me, but those are my clothes."

She smiled sheepishly. "Oh, I'm sorry, I thought someone left a present for me."

I surely wasn't expecting that kind of response from someone in the psyche ward. I half expected her to go crazy, but she didn't. When she came out of the bathroom with my clothes and handed them to me, she apologized again. I accepted her apology, changed into my clothes then wandered out into the hallway to look for a water fountain. As I walked towards the recreation room, I saw something that I will always remember — a beautiful young girl with long, black hair sitting on the floor rocking back and forth and humming to herself. There were other patients sitting around doing various things as well; either talking to each other or talking to themselves.

A woman's voice startled me and I turned around. It was the nurse.

"Ah Ivette, you're awake. The doctor will see you shortly."

I told her okay and I went back to my room. Shortly afterwards, the doctor came to my room to get me and we walked back towards his office.

When I sat down, he asked me what I thought were idiotic questions like what day it was, who was the President and what year it was. I couldn't figure out why he would ask me these questions. He was the doctor — didn't HE know who the President was? We talked briefly about why I was there and why I wanted to kill myself. I figured this was my time to finally tell someone with some authority and without interference from Victor about the abuse.

"My husband has been verbally and physically abusing me for some time and I can't get him to stop," I told him.

The look on his face gave me the impression he didn't believe me.

"According to your husband, Ivette, you have a tendency to blow things out of proportion. Besides, he said you two just had a marital spat. He feels that you are emotionally unstable and have a tendency to exaggerate."

Fuckin' people! Was everybody on drugs? Why didn't anyone believe that Victor was doing these things to me? I was reporting the abuse to someone in a position of authority, someone who was in a position to help me and he thinks I'm blowing things out of proportion or exaggerating the situation! I was frustrated to the point of tears because Victor played mind games with these people and they couldn't see it. And, I knew that if I started crying, it would confirm the doctor's belief that I was "mentally unstable." I didn't want to say what I thought, so I decided to phrase my response differently.

"Doctor, I do not have a tendency to blow things out of proportion. He's been doing these things to me for quite a while. What makes you think I would lie about something like that?"

Just as I finished my sentence, the doctor looked towards the door where Victor stood and put his hand up. The doctor never answered my question.

"Victor, just a minute," the doctor said.

I came to realize that because Victor was in the military, he was automatically given respect. Once he turned on the "charm," there was no way that the doctor would believe he could be capable of abuse.

I was angry that no one believed me — not the emergency room doctor, not the doctor in the psychiatric ward. As the doctor stepped out into the hallway to talk to Victor, I sat in the chair and became engrossed in my thoughts until the doctor interrupted me.

"I just spoke to your husband, Ivette. He has assured me that he doesn't want to leave you here and that he wants to take you home, provided that you behave yourself and don't try this again."

I gave the doctor a dumbfounded look. Then Victor interrupted as usual, always trying to be in control of everything.

"Doctor, can I talk to my wife for a minute?"

The doctor stepped out of his office to give Victor and me some privacy. I wanted to scream and curse him out, but thought better of it because this was not the place for that. They would certainly think I was "crazy" for sure, so I kept my mouth shut and rolled my eyes up at him. With a twisted smile on his face, Victor whispered to me, but talked loudly enough so the doctor could hear.

"Now Ivette, the doctor wants to keep you here another three days. I have the power to leave you here for the whole time, but I told him I want you home. Now, if you're not going to behave yourself or if you're going to act up and not listen to me, all I have to do is give the word. Now, are you going to behave yourself?"

My face went blank. I wanted to grab the stapler off the doctor's desk and slam it into his head. However, that wasn't going to help my situation. I had to go along with Victor's game, so I shook my head in agreement. I didn't belong there and had to do whatever it took to get out of there. Victor walked out of the office into the hallway towards the doctor.

"She'll behave herself, doctor. If she acts up again, I'm bringing her back."

I quietly walked out of the doctor's office and back to my room. As I packed my things, I thought about what I needed to do. I needed to get away from all of this, but where was I going to go? So far, I'd told the doctor about the abuse and half expected that he would be able to help me, only to be labeled as "crazy." I didn't have any money to leave my husband, but I couldn't live like this much longer. All I knew is that I had to do something real soon.

On our way back home, I sat in the car and didn't say a word. I didn't want to give Victor the slightest reason to turn the car around and take me back to that God-forsaken place. Victor didn't say anything either. We finally got back home and I dropped my bags on the floor and plopped on the couch.

"I called your mother and told her what happened. She wants you to call her as soon as you get home." Victor said.

I sighed and rolled my eyes up to the ceiling because now I had to explain this to my mother and I knew she wouldn't understand either. As I walked past him towards the phone to call my mother, I asked Victor a question.

"Why didn't you just let me die? Why couldn't you just leave me alone?" He had that twisted smile on his face again as he answered me.

"Because I wouldn't be able to explain to your family why you killed yourself. Besides you have ME to thank for saving your life and getting you out of the hospital. If it wasn't for me, you'd still be in there."

That arrogant bastard! This man had a lot of nerve. Him and his power trips! While I talked to my mother, Victor sat down on the couch and listened to my conversation.

"Hi Ma, it's me," I said when she answered the phone.

"Ivette, what happened? Are you starting to lose your mind? Are you having a nervous breakdown? Victor told me you two had an argument and then you took some pills," she said.

My mind went back to the time when my mother told Victor when we first got married that I couldn't take too much stress. I knew exactly where this conversation was going, so I decided to tell her about the abuse.

"Ma, Victor has been hitting on me. I'm tired of the nasty things he says to me and I'm tired of him hurting me." Her response didn't surprise me at all.

"Well you know what the Bible says about turning the other cheek.

You know the Bible and you know that a wife is supposed to be subservient to her husband." My mother quoted scripture after scripture until I cut her off.

Her response was the reason why I didn't want to tell her anything in the first place. I felt like Victor was using her to manipulate me again.

"Ma, please show me in the Bible where it says a husband is supposed to beat his wife or that a wife is supposed to be abused by her husband. I can only turn the other cheek but so much. There are only two sides to my face and he's already started kicking my ass."

As Victor sat on the couch and listened to my conversation, his constant snickering really annoyed me. I didn't like the fact that he was always trying to use my mother to manipulate me and it made me angry that she couldn't see it.

"Just try to be a good wife so he doesn't have anything to complain about. Things will get better, I'm sure. You can win him over by being a good Christian wife."

I didn't want to spend the rest of my life trying to please Victor, only for him to abuse me in return. That's not living — that's a nightmare! After listening to my mother and watching Victor stifle a laugh, I realized I wasn't crazy after all. Everyone else around me was.

Right after Victor locked up every drug in the house, he began to act lovey-dovey towards me, which could only mean one thing — he wanted sex.

"Come sleep in the bedroom," he said.

I looked at him in disgust and just shook my head. As I reluctantly went into the bedroom, I was torn between performing my "duty" as a wife and wanting to get out of this horrible situation. When he was done, I felt sick to my stomach.

Although my suicide attempt left me quiet and withdrawn, it gave me time to analyze my situation and figure out a way to improve it. I didn't want to bring children into the world with Victor treating me the way he did. He didn't want me to take birth control and if I went to the hospital to get it anyway, he would find out. So, I decided to resume my job search so I could save up enough money to leave him once and for all.

The next day, I applied for a job at Burger King. I could never see myself flipping burgers, but it was a job and I needed the money to get away from Victor. Within a week, I was working at Burger King for $3.25 an hour.

I was glad for the few hours I was out of the house and away from Victor's watchful eye, but when he got home from work, he expected dinner to be on the table as usual. I kept quiet and did what I could to please him to minimize conflict. When I finished cooking, I served him first and then sat down to eat, as I was taught to do.

"Can you get me the salt?" Victor asked.

I set my plate down and got up to get him salt, then sat back down to eat.

"Can you get me some more to drink?" It was as if he was doing this on purpose.

I set my plate down again, got Victor something to drink and sat down again to eat. By then, my food was cold and I didn't want to eat it anymore, so I threw it in the garbage.

Although I worked part-time, he expected me to give him my entire paycheck to pay the bills in the house and I simply refused to do that. Instead, I contributed what I could because I knew if Victor had the chance, he would take all my money and keep his money for himself.

Victor didn't let up with the verbal abuse, either. He constantly said that I was "flat-chested," then would cut out ads from the newspaper about breast enhancement surgery and leave them around the house. After a while, I believed my situation wasn't going to get any better and that wives were supposed bear the cross of her husband's cruel and inhuman treatment.

After working at Burger King for two weeks, I felt nauseous in the morning, only to be okay by the time I got to work. Figuring that maybe Victor gave me another infection, I asked Tracey if she would take me to the military hospital to have myself checked out. The doctor examined me, asked the usual health questions, asked me about my period, then said he would give me a pregnancy test.

"It's positive," the doctor said.

Chapter 9

Winter 1986 — And Baby Makes Three

After Tracey dropped me off at home, I wondered how I was going to tell Victor I was pregnant. I've always loved kids and was happy that I was about to be a mother. I felt that Victor would be too selfish and self-centered to be happy about being a father. But when he came home and dropped his bag on the floor, I just blurted it out.

"I'm pregnant."

Victor stood there and smiled. "Really?"

"Yes," I said.

He kissed me and said, "I'm so happy! Let's just keep this as our little secret for a while before we tell anybody." I was completely baffled!

For a brief moment, I felt like everything was going to be okay between us and things were happening like I thought they were supposed to happen. I thought to myself that Victor wasn't so bad after all. I guess he'd been under a lot of pressure from being in the military. I hoped that being pregnant would mean that Victor would start treating me better and stop hitting me.

The following week, I noticed Victor on the phone talking to his mother, telling her that I was pregnant. So much for it being "our little secret." I stood in front of Victor and overheard his mother's response.

"Oh, she's got you now," was all she said.

I was shocked that she would say something like that! She wasn't the slightest bit happy for us. How dare she think that I tried to get pregnant just to trap her precious son? I could see her feeling that way if

I got pregnant before we got married, but that wasn't the case. Victor didn't bother to tell her about our conversation about him not wanting me to get on birth control. Once again, I walked away shaking my head while he laughed and talked with his mother. I always thought something was seriously wrong with their relationship because it was unlike anything I'd ever seen. Oh well, despite what Susan said, I was happy about my pregnancy, even if no one else was.

Victor surprised me one day and said he wanted me to quit my job at Burger King.

"I want you to stay home and have a healthy baby," he told me.

Maybe this pregnancy was starting to have a positive effect on him after all. So, I quit my job and stayed home, feeling that Victor, as the head of the household, would take care of me. After all, he did want me to quit my job because he was concerned about the baby and me. It looked as if everything started to work out between us — he treated me better, even asked me if I wanted things. He seemed genuinely happy and concluded that maybe what we went through was just a rough patch. Every marriage has them, right? But other things did not change; he still wanted his dinner by a certain time and still wanted sex. However, in my mind, this was what being married was all about.

It didn't take long for Victor to get back into his old habits like going out of the house on the weekends, staying out all day, coming home late at night and leaving me in the house by myself. This time it didn't bother me because I had the baby to focus my energies on instead of what Victor was or wasn't doing. After a while, I cared less and less about Victor being out of the house. I hoped that he would leave me for good and was disappointed when I heard his key in the door. So what if his mother thought my being pregnant meant that I trapped her son? Of course, I didn't put it all together until much later, but I figured she said that because she tried to trap HIS father when she got pregnant with Victor at sixteen.

Of all the things Victor told his mother, he never told her that as long as I was barefoot and pregnant, he would always know where I was. At the end of the day, I didn't care what Susan thought of me. I knew that Victor told her a story that was definitely different from the truth. Moreover, it wasn't my place to convince Susan of anything anymore. Deep down, she knew he was abusing me and instead turned a blind eye, preferring instead to see her son as blameless. Susan never acknowledged that her son was an abuser and I doubt she ever will. Abusive men have two faces; one that they show their family and friends and people who they care about, and the other face they show to the survivor.

Despite all that was happening at home, Tracey was happy when she heard that I was pregnant. It helped keep my spirits up when she called to check up on me and stopped by when she knew that Victor was out of the house.

Chapter 10

Spring 1987 — Pulling Out the Rug

By April, my belly was getting bigger and I needed bigger clothes. I was not in the habit of asking Victor for money, but since he wanted me to quit my job, I thought he wouldn't have a problem with it.

"Victor, I need a few dollars to go to the mall and get some underwear. Mine are getting too small for me."

"I don't have any money," he said.

"But you just came in the house with some new records. Underwear doesn't cost that much." I knew Victor was selfish, but this was a bit much.

"How much you need?" he asked. I told him ten dollars.

"That's too much money. Besides, I ain't got it."

Right at that moment, I felt like he was slowly starting to pull the rug out from under me. I was so sick of Victor's shit. I walked past him right to the phone and called my mother.

"Hi Ma, it's Ivette," I began.

We talked for a few minutes with her asking me how I was. I had told her several weeks prior that I was pregnant and she seemed happy for me.

"I'm fine. Ma, I don't have any money to buy some underwear. Would you mind sending me a few dollars?"

"Well, where's Victor?" she asked.

"He's sitting right here. I asked him for it and he said he didn't have it."

Right away, Victor turned red. My mother hesitated for a few seconds and then sighed.

"Sure, I'll send you some money. You'll have it in a few days."

"Thanks Ma. I'll call you when I get it."

Then I hung up the phone and sat down at the dining table, looked at the TV and completely ignored Victor. Out of the corner of my eye, I saw him coming at me.

"How fuckin' dare you make me look bad like that to your mother! "I'm the man of this house. Now your old bat of a mother thinks I can't take care of my family!" he screamed.

The reality of the situation was, he was too selfish to take care of his family. I said nothing as I got up and walked away from him towards the bedroom. Then he grabbed me by the arm.

"Don't you dare walk away from me!" he yelled.

I pushed him away from me.

"Let me go!" I screamed.

Then Victor grabbed me from behind, pushed his knees into the back of my legs and pulled me backwards onto the floor. When he did, I fell flat on my back. That was the first time I actually noticed that under the carpet of our apartment was concrete and there was no padding underneath. He straddled my stomach and pinned my shoulders to the floor. The hard floor hurt my back and I pulled a muscle in my abdomen.

"I'm sick and tired of you! You're always trying to fuckin' make me look bad to everybody!"

Victor cared more about what other people thought of him than his own wife. I tried to get up but couldn't push him off of me for fear of injuring my baby.

"Get off me!" I screamed.

He kept me pinned to the floor by my shoulders.

"I'll fuckin' kill you!" he yelled back.

After he screamed and cursed at me for a few more minutes, he got up and went back on the couch. I tried to get myself off the floor slowly so I wouldn't hurt myself or my baby. I slowly rolled over to my side and pushed myself onto my knees. Then I pulled myself up, walked towards the bedroom and closed the door. I laid down on the bed, cried and thought things hadn't changed after all.

A few days later, I got the money my mother promised me. Of course, Victor had to be in control of everything, including the mail, so he knew when I got the money my mother sent. He stood over me while I opened the envelope from my parents.

"You know, since you got money, there's a few bills in this house that need paying," he said.

"Hmm, interesting," I said.

I paid him no mind. I needed underwear and that was what I was going to get. After all, he wanted to be the boss by telling me to quit my job.

"I'm going to the store and get myself some underwear that fits."

It seemed that Victor always wanted to control whatever I had, as if he couldn't stand someone else besides him having anything of value. It wasn't long before he came at me with new insults.

"You're not pregnant, you're fat. All you do is waddle around here and eat up my food. That can't be my baby — it must be the mailman's child."

I tuned him out and was determined not to let his insults bother me. It was the only way I could survive his abuse and have a healthy baby. I was about to be a mother and tried desperately to keep myself calm so my baby would be calm. Victor had some strange ways I didn't understand and I started to believe that I wasn't the one with the problem. I know I'm not a bad person and was raised to do unto others as I would have them do unto me, but I could never understand why Victor treated me as horribly as he did. I felt like I had nothing left but my faith in God and even that was starting to get a little shaky. Nevertheless, I didn't care what my religion said. I needed to strengthen my faith in God to carry me through this bad part of my life. I managed to find a Kingdom Hall in North Carolina and attended on a regular basis. Once I did, Victor did everything in his power to try to stop me.

"You are not raising my child in that kooky religion of yours," he said.

"So who's going to teach it about God and the Bible? It's not like you go to church," I replied.

It was bad enough that Victor abused me verbally and physically. Now, he was abusing me spiritually by making me feel that going to the Kingdom Hall was a privilege that I had to earn.

I only went to Kingdom Hall once a week and Victor played games like taking the car before I was about to leave or hiding the car keys. I defied him one day by walking the mile to the Kingdom Hall and people were nice enough to give me a ride home. God always makes a way for those who want to serve Him. Victor didn't seem too happy to know that I was going anyway, let alone to see me getting out of a strange car.

At Cambridge Arms, there was a problem with stray cats in the complex and sometimes they would jump on our window screen and tear it. That seemed to agitate Victor.

"I'm gonna get something for those damn cats and we're going to the mall so I can get an air gun."

I didn't understand why Victor had to be so destructive. I learned years later that there is a strong connection between domestic violence and animal abuse

"Why don't you leave those cats alone? They're not bothering us."

Victor wasn't listening to me. Our Siamese cat liked to sit in the window in the sun and I figured the cats were trying to get at her. Victor was determined to get an air gun and I couldn't talk him out of it, so we left the house and drove to the mall to get the gun. I found it surprising, like most things Victor did, about how he could want to buy an air gun when he wouldn't give me money to buy underwear. After walking around the mall for some time, I got tired and was ready to go home, but knew I couldn't until Victor was ready. When we finally got back home, Victor busied himself playing with his new air gun. I set up the targets that came with the gun throughout the house so he wouldn't damage anything. Soon, everything was full of copper pellets — picture frames, books, even the paneling. However, I didn't see Victor going outside to shoot at the cats. I sat down at the dinette table and watched TV while he shot up everything in the house. A few minutes later, he came to the dinette table. I was tired from the pregnancy and was glad for the opportunity to finally sit down. Victor sat across from me with the air gun, turned it around in his hands and then pointed it in my face.

"What would you do if I shot you right now?"

I thought that there was no way this person was serious, pointing a high-powered CO_2 air gun at his wife, his PREGNANT wife, the one who loved him so much!

"Victor, get that thing out of my face before it goes off!"

I noticed he didn't move his finger off the trigger and when he stretched out his arm, it covered the width of the table which was about 48" or so in diameter. Then he repeated himself.

"I said, what would you do if I shot you right now?"

I didn't like the tone of his voice and was getting scared that he would really shoot me in the face. I turned my chair around and put my back to him.

"Victor, don't do that! Stop playing!"

POW! Then I felt a burning sensation in my back. I thought to myself, please God let this be sweat running down my back! I put my hand under my shirt to feel where he shot me, rubbed my back and pulled out my hand. It wasn't sweat like I had hoped. It was blood. Victor laughed hysterically. He laughed so hard he couldn't contain himself.

I walked towards the kitchen, steamed that he had the nerve to shoot me with that stupid air gun. I was hell-bent on getting a frying pan to knock the shit out of him. I couldn't believe he actually shot me and even worse, he thought it was funny! Victor got up from the table and walked behind me to stop me from going to the kitchen.

"You're not going to hit me. I just wanted to see what you would do if I shot you."

"Let me go and I'll be more than happy to answer your question!" I said to him.

He blocked my way so I couldn't go into the kitchen. This is not the time to be fighting, I told myself. I was trying to be careful since I was pregnant. So I broke from Victor's grasp and went to the bathroom to wipe the blood off my back and get a band aid. I went into the living room and sat down with my arms folded, seething. For some reason Victor thought that was the time to talk to me.

"Aw c'mon, it's just a little hole. It'll heal up."

I felt so helpless because I couldn't do anything to protect myself. I was pregnant and if I challenged him, I could risk hurting myself and losing my baby. On the other hand, I couldn't just stand there and let him hurt me. My baby had no one to protect it but me. What kind of mother would I be if I couldn't protect my child?

I knew that since Victor was in the military, it meant he had easy access to guns. I was beginning to worry if the next time he would shoot me with the real thing.

Chapter 11

Summer 1987 — Victoria

It was July and since I was due to have my baby the following month, my doctor's visits were down to every two weeks. I didn't want Victor going with me to the doctor because if he cared about me and the baby, he wouldn't do the things he did to me. The doctor told me that both of us were fine and that I would hold on for a couple more weeks. However, when I went back home, I had a burst of energy and cleaned everything I could get my hands on. I then realized I had to hurry and cook dinner because Victor was on his way home. After we ate, the excessive cleaning finally caught up with me so I sat down on the couch. I felt pressure in my belly and the baby moved around a lot. I told Victor about the contractions, but he wasn't too excited because I had several instances of false labor and he thought that was what it was. Then the contractions came more frequently and wouldn't slow down. Then it dawned on me; it was time for me to go to the hospital because the baby was coming! I told Victor so and he reluctantly got up and got his car keys. He told me that if this was another case of false labor, he was going to make the hospital keep me.

About a half an hour later, Victor and I finally arrived at the hospital. I wasn't dilated enough so they made me walk around the hospital to help things along. After a few more hours, they finally admitted me and put me in a prep room where they could hook me up to a machine that monitored my contractions. The labor pains were excruciating! I asked Victor to get the nurse to get me something for the pain. As quickly as Victor left the room, he came back.

"The nurse said you shouldn't have anything for the pain — it's going to slow down the delivery."

I grabbed Victor by his collar.

"Go out of this fuckin' room, get the nurse and don't come back until you do!"

Victor walked out of the room backwards, looking at me as if I had three heads. But, when he came back, he had the nurse with him and, lo and behold, she had a syringe in her hand! She injected the liquid into my intravenous line and I felt it when the medication hit my veins. Moments later, the labor pains slowly subsided and I drifted off to sleep for what seemed like hours.

I was so naïve that when I woke up, I thought I had delivered the baby.

"Is the baby here yet?" I asked Victor, only to look at my belly and see that I was still pregnant.

"Damn" I said.

Stupid me, what did I know? I had no idea what childbirth would be like! I hoped it would be magical and painless. The joke was on me! Victor showed me the paper that recorded my contractions. I saw places where the needle came right off the page and I slept right through it!

"I had to put the needle back on the paper," he told me.

He ran out of the room to tell the nurse I was awake. The doctor did a final examination of me.

"She's fully dilated!" he said.

When it was time for me to go to the delivery room, I was surprised that Victor was right there with me. The nurses got me onto the delivery table and fully prepped. When the doctor told me to push, I pushed. I pushed and kept pushing while the doctor talked to me.

"You're doing great Ivette; the baby's head is out!"

Victor supported my back until he heard the doctor say the baby's head was out. Then let me fall down as he ran around to the front of the table to see what was going on.

"The baby's not completely born yet and the eyes are open!" Victor exclaimed, his face beaming with pride. Then, his demeanor changed.

"Why is this baby white with grey eyes?" He said.

With my legs still up in the air in the stirrups, everyone stopped what they were doing and looked at me!

"I haven't even seen my baby yet! Can I finish having it first?" I yelled.

After what seemed like hours of pushing, the baby finally arrived, six pounds and twenty-one inches long. I was so glad she was okay, beautiful and healthy. We named her Victoria.*

Three days later, it was time for Victoria and me to be discharged from the hospital. Victor was downstairs taking care of the discharge papers while I packed and got Victoria ready to go home. The little money I had saved from the brief time I worked was spent on baby clothes and anything else I wanted and needed for my baby. I put a cute little outfit on her, bundled her up, grabbed my bag and headed downstairs. At the time, there was a fee of seven dollars a day for my hospital stay, which came up to twenty-one dollars. Victor stood at the cashier's window and seemed a bit agitated. He was talking to himself.

"Do you have the money to pay for this?" he asked.

I couldn't believe that my husband was so cheap, he wouldn't pay twenty one dollars for my hospital stay! I told him I didn't and that he was the one who wanted me to quit my job, stay home and have a healthy baby. I did my part; now it was time for him to do his part, which was pay the hospital bill! He mumbled something under his breath as he pulled the money out of his wallet and slammed it on the counter. I really didn't care about what he was mumbling about. I knew Victor could easily spend twenty dollars on records, but I guess having Victoria wasn't going to change his attitude towards me after all. When we got home, his co-workers eventually stopped by that day to drop off baby gifts and fawn over Victoria. I was tired, wanted to sleep, and wasn't interested in entertaining any of Victor's friends. I wasn't the least surprised that he neither mentioned it to me or asked me if I was up for the company. By the end of the night after everyone left, Victor started in on me. He stood over Victoria's crib looking at her.

"That's not my child," he said.

"What are you talking about? Of course that's your child!" I said.

"She doesn't look anything like me. You were just sitting at home, not working. You were telling me you were looking for a job and I don't know if that's true. For all I know, you could have been having an affair with the mailman!"

Of all the things he could have said to me, I think that was the worst and the craziest. He was so upset that he walked over to the phone and called my parents to tell them Victoria and I were home. When my father picked up the phone, he whined to him.

"She don't look nothin' like me. She looks white, has blond hair and grey eyes," Victor told my father, sounding as if he was at the brink of tears.

Then I heard my father's voice, "Ivette was born just like that, and her eye color changed. Victoria got those traits from my side of the family."

My father's response did little to calm Victor down. As I spoke to my parents for a while, Victor gave me dirty looks. My father was so happy when Victoria was born that he called her Vicky and said he couldn't wait to see her. Afterwards, I spoke to my mom and put the phone to Victoria's ear so she could hear her. After I hung up from my parents, I went towards the bedroom with Victoria to get her ready for bed. I asked Victor to watch her while I got a bath ready.

"I ain't watchin' nobody else's child," he replied.

I just sighed and hoped he would get over it. Deep down inside, I knew Victor knew he was Victoria's father, but he just wanted to torture me as usual. After that, Victor did nothing to help me with the baby. He rarely held her and really didn't interact with Victoria like I thought a proud father should.

Despite dealing with Victor's childish and selfish behavior, I enjoyed taking care of and bonding with my baby. I never hesitated to kiss her and tell her how much I loved her. In addition, I made a promise to her that she would have the best life I could give her, even if that meant living a life without Victor.

Some weeks later, Victor mentioned to me that he had applied for on-post housing because living in a one bedroom with a baby wasn't good enough for him. So, that meant we were moving soon. Once again, I hoped that a change in scenery and a new environment would help my marriage. Despite everything that happened, I still held out hope that the light bulb would go off in Victor's head and things would get better for us. As it turned out, Victor was up to his old tricks again, staying out of the house on the weekends and constantly verbally abusing me. The days I spent at home alone with my baby caused me to reflect on my life, what I wanted for myself and what I wanted for my daughter. I tried to use that time alone to my advantage to sort through things. Although I still loved him in my own way, I realized I had to start thinking about leaving Victor if I was to get anywhere in my life with my daughter. But I was scared to take Victoria and leave. He treated Victoria and me as if we were nothing more than possessions to him. He threatened that if I left him, I wouldn't be taking the baby with me. Somehow, having Victoria motivated me to think about things I hadn't considered before. I didn't love him as much as I used to, but I didn't want to live my life fighting Victor off with one hand and raising Victoria with the other one either. The truth of the matter was, he never stopped abusing me and things were never going to get better. I didn't want my daughter to grow up and watch me be abused like that. And more importantly, I didn't want my daughter growing up thinking that it was acceptable for anyone to be treated like that. However, as long as I felt a little bit of love for Victor, I held out hope for our marriage. I felt that if I tried harder to make him happy, he would love me more and stop being abusive.

Victor caught onto the fact that I was doing whatever I could to make him happy and used that to his advantage. One night after I put Victoria to sleep, he wanted sex. I told him I couldn't until I went back for my six-week checkup.

"You won't get pregnant," he said.

I tried to push him away, but as usual, he kept pestering me until I gave in and that happened several times.

By the end of August, it was time to go back to the doctor for my six-week checkup.

"Everything seems fine and you're healing well," the doctor said.

That was, until he pressed down on my stomach.

"Something doesn't seem right here," he said.

He called in another doctor for a second opinion. He said something didn't feel right either. The doctor called for the nurse to bring him the sonogram machine. Victor stayed at the office with me watching everything and Victoria was sleeping in her stroller. The doctor hooked me up to the sonogram machine and turned out the light. He moved the wand back and forth on my belly to get an image on the screen.

"Just what I thought, you're pregnant." Then I heard a crash.

The doctor quickly turned on the light and I saw Victor on the floor talking to himself.

"Oh shit! Not again! I don't believe it!"

I was in shock. What was I going to do?

The doctor cut off my train of thought.

"It is either the overshadowing of a really big baby or you're having twins. But, I'll stake my reputation on it that it's twins."

The only other twins born in my family were from my grandmother. Then Victor interrupted the doctor.

"Shit, I can see everything in triples. Oh, shit! There goes all my money!"

I tried not to think about Victor and how he felt. I was having two more babies and my due date was June 1988.

As soon as we left the doctor's office and got into the car, Victor brought up the subject about having an abortion.

"We can't afford three children," he said.

"You know I don't believe in abortion. You should have thought about that before having sex with me without a condom when I told you I could still get pregnant," I shot back.

"The day I have to use a condom with my WIFE is the day I have no more use for you," Victor said.

Victor felt he could do whatever he wanted to me with no consequence. Did he really think he could pester me to have an abortion like he pestered me to have sex with him?

It seemed that every time Victor laid his eyes on me, he talked to me about having an abortion. The more I said I wasn't having one, the angrier he got. I was of the mind that I would sooner raise three children by myself than raise one child with Victor and feel guilty about aborting not one, but two babies. I couldn't believe what he was asking me to do. I put my foot down with him that I wasn't having an abortion and that was that. I had to get used to the fact of giving birth to three children within a year and raising them with or without him.

Victor came home from work one day with what I thought was good news.

"We've been invited to an outing tomorrow with the guys from the base and their families," he told me.

On occasion, I saw glimmers of hope that my marriage was going to work and it made me believe that I could stay with Victor. Being excited that this would be the first time we actually went out as a family was one of those glimmers. That is, until the glimmer turned to gloom. Saturday finally came and we packed up Victoria and drove to the park where everyone was sitting. When we got there, I saw all the guys in one area of the park with their families congregated together at the picnic tables. When Victor and I got there, the guys and their wives said "Hi" to him, but no one said anything to me. I thought it was strange that he didn't bother introducing me to the wives. I stood there awkwardly holding Victoria and looked at everyone while Victor walked off to be with the guys. Still, no one said anything to me. I noticed some swings off to the side of the park, so I went there and played with Victoria. I didn't learn until many years later that the reason why no one spoke to me was because Victor told everyone beforehand that I was mentally unstable, that I had tried to commit suicide and that no one should say anything to me for fear of "setting me off." He wanted to keep me isolated and didn't want me to have any more "friends" like Tracey. I didn't care anymore what Victor did or said about me. It was about my baby and me.

Since we would soon be moving on base, Victor and I looked for new furniture while we lived at Cambridge Arms so we could have it delivered to the new apartment. I learned not to make too many plans for the future because I had to enjoy my non-violent days with Victor one day at a time. We looked around for furniture — rather Victor looked, because I didn't have any money to buy anything. It seemed like hours that I followed Victor around the store with Victoria and I was getting tired and wanted to go home. Victor didn't like anything in the store so we started to leave. Therefore, Victor walked out one exit and I was about to walk out the other.

"Go this way because it's shorter," Victor told me.

"It looks like the car is parked nearer to this exit," I said back to him.

I walked out the door anyway and made it to the car before he did. In a move that reminded me of when I was sixteen and Victor hit me for the first time in Central Park, I saw him look around as if he was checking for someone or something. I looked around too, trying to see what he was looking at, but saw nothing. I did however notice another couple leaving their car and going into the furniture store. The guy had on fatigues and I noticed Victor looking at him. As I took Victoria out of her stroller to put her in her car seat, Victor charged around the car to where I was standing with Victoria. He screamed to the top of his lungs, just enough to catch the attention of the couple about to walk into the store.

"When I tell you to walk in a certain direction, that is the way you walk! You don't walk the way YOU want to! I told you my way was shorter!"

This man has lost his goddamn mind, I thought. That was when I turned around and saw the couple had stopped walking and was staring at us.

"What difference did it make which way I walked? If I remember correctly, I beat you to the car, so your way wasn't shorter!" I spat back.

I was tired of Victor not only trying to embarrass me in public, but also talking to me like that while I held Victoria.

"Get in the fuckin' car!" he yelled.

I calmly got into the car and made up my mind that I would deal with him when we got home. I stayed quiet as a mouse, because for all I knew, he would drive off the road and kill all of us. All the while, my anger built up and I was determined to let him have it when we got in the house. We finally got home and I put Victoria in her crib. I had had enough of his bullshit.

"Who the fuck do you think you are talking to me in the street like that!!? Motherfucker, you have lost your goddamn mind! Now you want to tell me which direction I should walk in? You wouldn't give me ten dollars to buy a pair of cheap underwear but you want to tell me which direction I should walk in? My father's name is the only man's name on my birth certificate! You stupid piece of worthless shit!"

I picked up one of his steel-toed combat boots and threw it at his head. He ducked and it bounced off the wall right into Victoria's crib, but it didn't hit her. I couldn't believe what I had just said and done but I was so angry from everything he had put me through. I was tired of "turning the other cheek," I was tired of the insults and if I was going to get my ass beat, it was going to be because I stood up for myself, not because I stood there and let him do it. I knew I was pregnant with twins, but I felt they would be okay, because I wasn't showing yet. I was ready to take him on!

He acted as if he didn't hear a word I said.

"You fucking bitch! You lost your mind? That boot almost hit my baby!" and he ran towards me like a linebacker.

For a quick minute, I realized he called Victoria "his baby."

"She ain't your baby. You told me she belonged to the mailman!"

I didn't care that I was antagonizing him. I wanted to rip his face off once and for all! He came at me and tried his signature move of putting his hand around my throat. We struggled, tussled, and grunted until we both fell on the floor.

"I'll kill you! he said.

"Not today, you won't!" I grunted back.

The only thing that snapped me out of trying to kill him was that Victoria started crying. I kicked him off of me and went over to Victoria's crib. I snatched the boot out of her crib and threw it back at Victor, trying to hit him in the head with it. I picked up Victoria and tried to calm her down. She was only three months old and if I only knew how much of an effect all this fighting and violence would have on her, I would have left sooner.

Chapter 12

Fall 1987 — Back to the Usual

As Victoria got bigger, I enjoyed every minute I could spend with her. By the time she was three months old and I was three months pregnant, we had already settled in a townhouse on base. It was a nice place located on Spear Drive and much better than our apartment at Cambridge Arms. It even had a nice front lawn that Victor refused to mow.

"I have to work every day. You don't have a job and that's the least you could do," Victor would say.

It didn't matter to Victor that not only did I have an infant to take care of, but that I was also pregnant with twins. The house on base was nice, with a decent sized living room and from there you could walk into the dining area and the kitchen. The kitchen had an eat-in area and access to the backyard. Upstairs, there were two bedrooms and a bathroom. One for Victor and me and the other bedroom would be for Victoria and the twins. Once again, I knew I couldn't rely on Victor to take care of Victoria and me, so I found a job working as a salesperson in the mall nearby and a twenty-four hour child care center for Victoria, which I was grateful for. In the meantime, Victor bought himself another car which was a two-door sporty model. Once again, I wondered where he got the money for the car since he couldn't give me ten dollars to buy underwear. I asked him why did he buy another car since he always said he didn't have any money.

"One car is for me to drive to work and the other car is for me to drive to the club," he said.

Here I am, pregnant with twins, taking care of a newborn and working and I wasn't allowed to drive either of the cars. Because my work schedule was so erratic, rather than let me drive one of the cars to work, Victor drove me to work and picked me up. But when my shift changed to evenings, he had no other choice but to reluctantly let me drive the other car.

The violence, insults and unkind words slowly dissolved the love I had for Victor. Although the doctors warned me that my second pregnancy was high risk, I decided that the only way Victoria and I would have anything was for me to continue to work. I spent countless hours on my feet at the department store, and then had to pick up Victoria from day care, sometimes as late as 10 p.m. When I asked Victor to pick Victoria up just to give me a break, he told me it didn't make sense to have two cars in one place. Instead, Victor would go home after work, relax and watch TV until I got home then wait for me to cook dinner. So much for a new life in a new home.

Since we lived on Fort Bragg, we didn't have to pay rent, light and gas. The only bill we were required to pay was our phone and cable bill and Victor paid that. With what little money I made at the department store, Victor tried to figure out ways take it from me.

"You know this bill needs to be paid," he would tell me.

Another benefit of working at the department store was that I was entitled to discounts on clothing and merchandise. Victor would say that he needed a new pair of pants for the club, a new shirt, or something else. I wasn't paying Victor any mind because my multiple pregnancies was Victor's way of keeping me "barefoot and pregnant" just so that he could keep tabs on me.

It wasn't long before Victor started going to the clubs again and leaving Victoria and me at home alone. Tracey would come by to keep me company while Victor was out and leave before he got home because we both knew he would get upset if he knew she was there. Being pregnant again forced me to think more about my life and what kind of future I wanted for my three children. After all that happened, I knew Victor was no longer a part of my future. I wanted so much for my children, and watching their mother being abused, degraded and humiliated was not one of them. I wanted them to grow up in a loving and secure home, even if that meant I was the only one raising them. I knew in my heart that I wouldn't be the first woman to raise kids by herself, nor the last. In order for my children and me to have some happiness our lives, I had to leave Victor. For the sake of our safety, I had to start planning my exit from this horrible marriage. I loathed Victor because he had neither conscience nor the slightest bit of remorse for what he was doing to his family.

Chapter 13

Winter 1988 — And Babies Make Five

My pregnancy with the twins was taking its toll on me physically and mentally. At five and a half months pregnant, I had trouble walking, sleeping, sitting and the worst case of indigestion. I still worked at the mall and my co-workers were very understanding about my condition and let me take extra breaks. I knew I would need as much money as I could possibly make because I was leaving Victor soon after the twins were born. Although I knew I was leaving Victor, I wasn't sure if I was going to stay in North Carolina and rebuild my life or go back to New York, but one thing was for certain; I had to leave.

Victor still refused to pick up Victoria from day care when I got off work and was still waiting for me at home to make dinner. I couldn't even rely on him to take Victoria for a little while so I could get some rest because Victoria wouldn't let him hold her. The abuse had an effect on her. If Victor got too close to me, she would cry and scream at the top of her lungs until he backed away. There were nights that after having to pick up Victoria from day care that I was so tired that I had to pull along the side of the road and sleep. I was so fed up with Victor's selfish, self-centered ways that I warned him that one day he was going to come home to an empty house if he didn't start treating me better.

"You'll never leave me. And if you do, I'll always find you. What ya gonna do, go to New York and find a boyfriend?" I blankly stared at him while he continued his tirade.

"You're old, fat, ugly and used up. You can't leave me! Nobody would want your ass."

"Well then, since you feel that way, what's one man's trash is another man's treasure," I responded.

Because I was determined to leave, what he said didn't seem to bother me. I was twenty-one years old and was about to have three children. I knew I wasn't old or fat — just pregnant and at my age, I definitely wasn't used up!

Being pregnant with twins meant I needed as much sleep as I could get before I went to work the next day. I said little to Victor for fear of his bringing up the subject of abortion again, which he knew I wasn't going to do. Sleep deprivation is a tactic the military uses to wear down the enemy. And that is what Victor did to me. He would talk to me until I fell asleep and then violently shake me to wake me up. Then he would ask me if I heard what he just said, as if he were a little child begging for his Mommy's attention. He would do that several times a night and the worst part was that he thought it was funny. By the morning, I was exhausted.

In looking through Victor's things one day, I found some letters he and his mother had written to each other. One letter in particular caught my attention. It was dated a month or so before Victor called off our wedding.

> "*Victor,*
> *I am happy to hear that you and Lisa are finally getting together, but what about your wedding to Ivette? If you knew you wanted to marry Lisa, you should have never asked Ivette to marry you....*"

My God! I knew it! I remembered the first love letter I found from Lisa and knew Victor called off the wedding because he couldn't have kids. But to know that Susan knew about it then lied to me was beyond belief. Seething, I marched over to the phone and called Susan.

"Susan, its Ivette. Remember when I talked to you about Victor calling off our wedding? You told me you didn't know why." Susan paused for a second.

"Yes, I remember telling you that. I told you I didn't know why Victor called off the wedding." At that moment, I knew I had caught her in a lie. What was done in the dark had come to light!

"Well, according to this letter you wrote, just before Victor called off our wedding, you told him you were happy that he was marrying Lisa."

Then I read her a few lines from the letter, including the part about me. Her silence spoke in volumes and I got angrier by the second.

"Susan, are you there? Why did you lie to me?"

"You and Victor need to talk," was all she said.

"Talk? What is there to talk about?"

"Here I am with one baby and two more on the way and still being abused by your son. I had a right to know the truth! You had a right to tell me so I could make my own decision! I left Victor alone after he called off the wedding. He came back and said he wanted to marry me but only after Lisa got stationed somewhere else! AND YOU KNEW EVERYTHING!"

Susan said nothing. Instead, she just hung up on me. I didn't even bother telling Victor about our conversation because I knew Susan would call him and tell him everything.

The more I realized that I had to get away from Victor, the less Victor's abuse seemed to bother me. He still annoyed the hell out of me by trying to convince me to get an abortion, even at five and a half months pregnant! Still, each time, I told him I wasn't doing it and that was that! He also knew that because of my religion, I did not believe in blood transfusions and considered it a sin. Praying that there was a shred of humanity left in him, I reminded him to not let me have a blood transfusion, even if it meant I would die. It was no surprise to me that he quickly agreed.

A few days later, I called my mom to see how she was doing and to let her know I was okay.

"You know Ivette, I've been thinking. You're going to have your hands full with the twins. I can watch Victoria up here in New York until you have the twins. After you've had the twins, I'll bring Victoria back to you and stay to help you for a while. But first, you talk it over with your husband."

I knew there was nothing to talk over with Victor, because he talked about her behind her back then smiled in her face.

"I will Ma and let you know."

I told Victor about my conversation with my mother when he got home. I had to do something to look out for myself because it was clear that Victor wasn't looking out for me.

"Your mother isn't taking Victoria anywhere!" he screamed.

I continued to plead with him.

"Victor, I need some rest. You're not helping me because you're always out partying. I can't keep walking up and down the stairs anymore. It's getting harder and harder for me to get around. I'm tired from working and you still expect me to come home and cook dinner for you. If my mother wants to help, I'm going to let her."

"Victoria isn't going any fuckin' where! If you want me to help you, I'll buy a small refrigerator and put it in the bedroom!" he yelled again.

I finally had had enough of Victor and was starting to lose my temper. I had to take a stand against Victor, if not for my sake, then for the sake of my children, for the sake of my health.

"I'm going to let my mother take Victoria and that's it!"

I was so frustrated and angry at his selfish ways, his lack of support, and his constant abuse that I flipped over a folding table with an alarm clock on it and stormed towards the stairs. Victor ran behind me, grabbed me by the arm and dragged me back into the bedroom. I tried to get away from him, but couldn't.

"You knocked over my fucking table? I told you about telling me what you're going to do!" Victor yelled.

I heard Victoria crying in the other bedroom. Victor spun me around so he could stand behind me then he put me in a combat chokehold, with the crook of his arm getting tighter around the front of my neck. Because I couldn't breathe, my chest burned and I felt dizzy. I also felt the twins moving around in my belly more than usual and it didn't feel right.

While I struggled to move Victor's arm from around my throat so I could take a breath, Victor whispered in my ear through clenched teeth, "You can't breathe now, can ya bitch!"

The more I struggled and tried to get his arms from around my neck, the more Victor tightened his grip. Not only did he tighten his grip around my neck, he used his height to bend backwards until he had lifted me off the floor with his arm still tight around my throat. When he pulled me backwards, my belly tightened and my back hurt because the twins were moving so much. I couldn't get my footing because my toes barely touched the floor.

I heard Victoria crying in the other room and I was powerless to get to her. This is it, I thought — he's really going to kill me because I wouldn't have an abortion! I prayed to God to help me when he finally released his grip around my neck and let me fall to the floor on my knees. I coughed uncontrollably, and tried to catch my breath so the dizziness would go away. Before I could get my bearings, Victor grabbed me again, yanked me up and pushed me towards the edge of the stairs. In the process, Victor pushed me into the wall and my shoulder hit the light switch. With whatever strength I had left, I fought Victor and tried to keep from being pushed down the stairs.

"Get off of me!" I screamed repeatedly.

I knew my babies and I would die if he succeeded in pushing me down the stairs. With Victoria still crying and screaming, all I could think about was getting away from Victor and getting to my baby. Our townhouse was attached to the house next door and I hoped that through the thin walls someone would hear me and come to help. However, no help came.

Just as suddenly as he started, he stopped. He stood there, sweaty and breathing hard when I ran towards our bedroom to pick up Victoria. Then he came back in the room.

"Nobody is taking my daughter!" he screamed.

In order to maintain control by keeping me from calling anyone or going anywhere, he grabbed his things, took both sets of car keys, all the phones in the house and left to go to work.

Victoria was so upset and cried so hard that for a while, I couldn't get her to calm down. I took her into my bedroom, sat down with her on the bed and rocked her back and forth.

"Mommy's okay baby," I said to her.

I thought about what I needed to do next. Victor took both sets of car keys, so I couldn't drive anywhere. He took all the phones out of the house so I couldn't call anyone. I knew there was a pay phone in the Post Exchange, the grocery store on base. I rummaged through my pocketbook and found some change. I walked to the store and called the Military Police. Then I called his company commander because this time, Victor had gone way too far!

I finally managed to calm Victoria down, but it was short-lived because when I put her down long enough to put my shoes on, she cried and screamed again. I needed to leave the house quickly so I could call the police before Victor backtracked on me, so I slung Victoria on my hip and walked to the Post Exchange. I didn't care if people stared at me with a swollen face from crying and being choked, my clothes disheveled, my hair a mess, pregnant and carrying a baby. When I arrived at the store, I called the Police first.

"I'm six-and-a-half months pregnant and I want to report that my husband just assaulted me." Then I gave them my address.

"We'll be there shortly, ma'am," the officer said.

Then I hung up and called Victor's company commander. I had to be clear about what I needed to say to him without crying. When he answered the phone, I took a deep breath.

"I told you before that Victor was hitting me and you never believed me. His other commanding officers knew that he was hitting me. Now I hope you'll believe me!"

He asked me what happened and I told him everything, including Victor taking the phones and the car keys. I was tired of Victor's abuse, tired of people not believing me, tired of living the way I was living. The company commander said nothing.

"It's a shame that you feel someone with no self-control who beats on a pregnant woman deserves rank," I said through tears. Then he cut me off.

"I'll have Victor come home immediately," he said.

Because the military had a "hands-off" policy regarding domestic violence, by sending Victor back home to "handle his business," his commanding officer put Victoria's and my safety at risk. The military had a credo: "If we wanted the service member to have a wife, we would have issued him one."

I was so frustrated with everything that I hung up on him. If I told the commanding officer that Victor assaulted me, why would he send him home? I was exhausted and angry. Once again, I tried to think of ways that I could get my child and myself away from him and be safe. I figured that no matter what happened to me, I was determined to make somebody listen. I had been silent for way too long.

The Police rang the bell not long after Victoria and I got home. I stood in the corner of the living room holding Victoria and telling them everything that happened. Victor walked in the door minutes later.

"What's the problem, officers?" he said matter-of-factly.

One of the officers responded.

"Your wife is alleging that you strangled and assaulted her."

I held Victoria and stood behind the other officer, hoping that this was one situation Victor couldn't lie his way out of.

"Now officers, as you can see, my wife is pregnant and very emotional. I would never treat her like that. Besides, you don't see any bruises on her, do you?"

The officers turned around and looked at me. I definitely didn't look like I'd stepped out of a fashion magazine. I hadn't combed my hair or changed my clothes.

"But he strangled me!" I yelled.

"Calm down, ma'am," one of the officers said sternly.

He acted as if I was annoying him. Here we go again, I thought. Then Victor walked closer to where the officers were standing.

"Officers, I'm sorry my wife wasted your time."

He shook hands with the officers and they left without asking me if Victoria and I were okay or if I wanted to go to the hospital. As the officers walked out before him, Victor turned around and gave me the most vile look before he walked out and closed the door. He still hadn't bothered to leave the other set of car keys or put the phones back in the house and the officers mentioned nothing about it before they left. Victoria still stuck to me like glue and I couldn't put her down, so I took my baby upstairs into her room, locked the door and lay down with her. I wasn't feeling well and thought the rest might help. I figured I would wait until Victoria went to sleep to take a shower and change my clothes. Of course, the moment Victoria went to sleep and I moved to get off the bed to go to the bathroom she woke up and started crying. I ended up taking her in the bathroom with me and hoped a warm shower would calm both of us down.

Later that day, just before Victor came home, I put Victoria in her stroller and took her for a walk around the block. I had hoped the walk would help clear my head and keep Victoria calm at the same time. When I came back, Victor was at home sitting in front of the TV and eating a sandwich. He acted as if nothing had happened.

"Give your mother a call," he said.

The tone of his voice meant that he had called my mother to "tell on me." I just walked past him to the phone and called my mother.

"What's going on with you two?" my mother asked.

I told her everything that happened that morning. Victor couldn't let me have a conversation with my mother in peace, so he yelled,

"I didn't do anything to her. I just got angry because she hadn't cooked in a while. I have to fend for myself!" Then he smiled.

What a pathological liar! He couldn't tell the truth if his life depended on it!

"Ivette, what did I say to you before about not giving Victor a reason to get on you? Victor tells me you haven't been cooking or cleaning or anything," she said.

I figured my mother was drinking from the same contaminated well Victor and his mother drank from. I didn't have time to listen to her chastise me and proceeded to tune her out. I was tired of everyone blaming me for what Victor did. I just cut her off in mid-sentence.

"Ma, I don't feel well. I told you what he did to me so I'm going to call an ambulance and go to the hospital to have myself checked out."

I wasn't in any pain but I just felt tired. She acted as if she didn't hear what I said which was typical of my mother. Whose side was she on anyway!

"Ma, I've been working full time. I have to pick Victoria up late at night from day care because Victor feels there shouldn't be two cars in the same place. When I come home, I'm tired and the last thing I want to do it wait on Victor hand and foot."

"Just let Victor take you to the hospital," my mother interjected, as if she didn't hear a word I just said.

"I don't want him anywhere near me!" I yelled.

I was tired of my mother taking Victor's side and not believing me and, believe me, that wasn't the first nor the last time.

"I'll take her to the hospital," Victor said into the air, hoping my mother would hear him. Then turned towards me and smiled again. He was still sitting on the couch, eating a sandwich and watching a basketball game, which meant I would have to wait until he was finished eating his sandwich and watching the basketball game. My mother heard him and responded to me.

"If Victor said he'll take you, let him take you!" my mother said in an authoritative tone.

"Fine! I gotta go Ma. Talk to you later."

I hung up and sat down at the dining room table still holding Victoria. As I predicted, I had to wait over an hour for Victor to finish his sandwich and for the basketball game to be over.

When Victor drove me to the military hospital, he left Victoria with me and said that he had to pull another shift at work and drove off. Nothing more, nothing less. I wasn't surprised because he knew what he did to me and he was running away like a punk. I took Victoria and proceeded into the emergency room. I spoke to the doctor on duty and told him about the assault and that I just wanted to have myself checked out. Dr. Marcus* quickly had a nurse escort me to an examining room and began the examination. That was one time I couldn't hold Victoria, so one of the nurses stayed in the room with me and held her.

"You've started dilating. We'll have to admit you right now. But your daughter isn't allowed upstairs. Is there anyone that you can call to take her?" he said.

"No, I don't have any family down here; my husband just dropped me and the baby off and then left." I told him.

The nurses were kind enough to take Victoria to the nurses' station while they admitted me. Once I was in a bed, they hooked me up to a sonogram machine to monitor my contractions.

"You're definitely in labor," Dr. Marcus said. I didn't understand what the doctor meant because I wasn't in any pain. I just felt tired.

While Dr. Marcus continued to examine me, he said, "Tell me again what happened today." Then he looked at my neck.

"What's that bruising around your neck?" I asked for a mirror and sure enough, there were broken blood vessels around my neck that looked like a necklace. He also noticed a nasty bruise had appeared on my left shoulder from where he pushed me into a light switch. I again gave the doctor a blow-by-blow account of what happened.

"Ivette, we have to stop your labor. It's too early for these babies to be born." He said to me.

The nurses came in and started an IV line. The nurse gave me medication intravenously and in pill form in order to stop my labor. The doctor came back into my room and I asked him how Victoria was doing.

"She's fine and at the nurse's station. They really love her," he said.

As I looked at the sonogram machine, I was amazed at what I saw on the screen. Even at 26 weeks pregnant, I could see my babies clearly. I watched them move around, with one of the babies putting a thumb in its mouth while taking the other hand and punching at the other baby. Then the other baby punched back. I could tell that they were fraternal twins and prayed to God that they would be okay.

"Just hold on a little while longer," I said to the monitor.

A few hours went by when I started to feel hungry. I called one of the nurses and was told that I was only allowed to eat ice chips, so she made sure I had plenty of them, which really annoyed the twins and me. As I ate the ice chips, I tried to imagine them as anything other than ice chips; a steak, a salad, or even a cheeseburger.

While I lay in the hospital, I started to feel a bit better and things seemed as if they would be all right and I could be discharged in the morning. After the last pill of the night, I felt sick to my stomach, so I got out of the bed, went to the bathroom and threw up the medication. It wasn't until I got back into the bed that I felt the pains. I frantically rang the bell by my bed for the nurse. Next thing I remember, the doctor and a couple of nurses ran into my room. I told them that I threw up the medication. The doctor quickly examined me.

"She's in full blown labor!" he yelled at the nurses.

"Get her up to the delivery room NOW!"

I remember my bed spinning and shaking as the nurses pushed me out the door towards the elevator.

I started crying, "Please not now! Don't take my babies now! It's not time! Oh God, please not now!"

I remembered feeling air in my face as the bed was quickly pushed into the elevator. While in the elevator, I blurted out that I was a Jehovah's Witness and that I didn't want a blood transfusion. I couldn't stop crying for the doctors not to take my babies. Where in the HELL was Victor? I thought.

A D D E N D U M

PETITIONER

---████████████████---

-VS-   DOCKET ████████

LETTIE IVETTE ███████   RESPONDENT

FAMILY OFFENSE PETITION

PETR, ████████████████ IS FILING THIS FAMILY OFFENSE PETITION AGAINST RESPONDENT,
LETTIE IVETTE ████████ HIS SPOUSE. PETR ALLEGES THAT ON MONDAY, JULY 10, 1989, AT
████████████████████████████████ RESP DID ENGAGE IN VIOLENT AND THREATENING BEHAVIOR.

PETR ALLEGES THAT HE WENT TO RESP HOME TO ATTEMPT TO VISIT WITH HIS CHILDREN. PETR ALLEGES
THAT HE SAT WITH THE CHILDREN IN RESP HOME AT RESP MOTHER'S REQUEST. PETR ALLEGES THAT
RESP WANTED TO DENY THE VISIT BUT RESP MOTHER REQUESTED THAT THE RESP ALLOW THE PETR TO
VISIT WITH THE CHILDREN. PETR ALLEGES THAT AFTER A WHILE PETR REQUESTED TO TAKE THE
CHILDREN OUT TO BUY ICE CREAM. PETR ALLEGES THAT RESP TOLD PETR THAT HE COULD NOT STAY TO
VISIT WITH CHILDREN UNLESS PETR PURCHASED CERTAIN ITEMS. PETR ALLEGES THAT WHEN HE REFUSED
TO PURCHASE THE ITEMS RESP WANTED, RESP THEN BEGAN TO FIGHT PETR. PETR ALLEGES THAT RESP
DID BITE PETR ABOUT THE FOREARM AND KICKED PETR SEVERAL TIMES. PETR ALLEGES THAT WHEN HE
COULD GET AWAY FROM RESP, PETR DID FILE A COMPLAINT WITH THE ████PRECINCT. PETR ALLEGES
THAT HE SOUGHT MEDICAL AIDE FROM ████████████ BROOKLYN, NY ON 7/11/89 BECAUSE THE RESP
HAD BROKEN PETR SKIN WHEN RESP BIT PETR ARM.* PETR ALLEGES THAT THE RESP DOES ALSO HARASS
PETR CONTINUOUSLY BY TELEPHONE WHEN PETR IS ON BASE IN NORTH CAROLINA. PETR ALLEGES THAT

*PETR ALLEGES THAT THE CHILDREN WERE PERSENT DURING THE CONFRONTATION BETWEEN PETR AND RESP.

RESP DOES CONTINUOUSLY TELEPHONE PETR COMMANDING OFFICERS AND COMPLAIN THAT SHE DOESN'T
RECEIVE SUPPORT MONIES, ETC. PETR ALLEGES THAT ALTHOUGH HIS COMMANDING OFFICERS KNOW OF
THE RESP PROBLEMS, ETC, THEY ARE STILL HARASSING PETR AS A RESULT OF RESP TELEPHONE CALLS.

PETR REQUESTS THAT RESP BE ORDERED NOT TO TELEPHONE PETR OR PETR COMMANDING OFFICERS WHILE
PETR IS ON BASE AT FORT BRAGG, NORTH CAROLINA. EPTR FURTHER REQUESTS THAT RESP BE ORDERED
TO ALLOW PETR TO VISIT WITH HIS CHILDREN AWAY FROM RESP HOME WHILE PETR IS ON LEAVE.
PETR REQUESTS AN ORDER OF PROTECTION.

████████████████████
PETITIONER

SWORN TO BEFORE ME ON THIS 12TH DAY OF JULY 1989.

_____
COURT ASSISTANT

I CERTIFY I HAVE BEEN GIVEN AN EXPLANATION
WITH RESPECT TO SECTION ██ AND ██6 OF THE
JUDICIARY LAW ████ ██████ ████ OFF-
ENSE AND SAME, ███ ████ ██████████ TO ME
AND I UNDERSTAND MY RIGHTS ██████████████
████████████████████
PETITIONER'

*Fig. 1 Victor petitioned the court for an Order of Protection after he assaulted me in my
mother's apartment.*

The New York Society for the Prevention of Cruelty to Children

REPORT OF INVESTIGATION

PRIVILEGED and CONFIDENTIAL
Submitted at the request of
Hon. Judge Kaplan

NYSPCC # ███████   Docket #███████████
                          Adjourned: 12/18/89

FAMILY COMPOSITION:

PETITIONER: ███ ████ █████████, FATHER, Fort Bragg, N.C.

RESPONDENT: LETTIE IVETTTE ████████, MOTHER, ████████████████████

CHILDREN: ██████████(d.o.b. ████);
          ██████████(d.o.b. ████); c/o Mother.

NATURE OF CASE:

The father filed for Visitation vs. Mother, on 7/12/89. The mother filed a Petition for Modification of a T.O.V. and an Order of Protection, on 7/13/89.

ISSUES:

The mother is not opposing visitation for the father but she would like a week's notice advising of the visit with the children. The father alleges, that the mother does not allow him visitation and has assaulted him.

CONTACTS:

9/26/89, Spoke with mother about scheduling an interview.

10/30/89, Contact letter was mailed to the mother.

11/13/89, Spoke to the mother.

11/14/89, Left name and number for the father at ███████████; Ft. Brag

12/01/89, Left name and number with Sgt. Sanchez, at Ft. Bragg for father

12/08/89, Officer interviewed the mother at her home.

12/11/89, Contact letter mailed to the father.

12/13/89, Officer left name and number with Sgt. Sanchez, for the father.

12/15/89

        On 12/5/89, officer visited the home of the mother, Lettie
Ivette ██████████ at ████████████████████████.

Fig. 2 - Report from the Society for the Prevention of Cruelty to Children presented to Judge Kaplan.

Ms. ▮ advised, that she is willing to allow visitation but she is against overnight visits as she feel the children are too young. The mother also advised, that she would like to have one week's notice that the father is coming to see the children on wEEKENDS. The mother stated, that she believes her husband is not genuinely interested in his children.

The mother feels this way because of the infrequency of his contact with his daughter. In 7/89, the mother alleges, the father saw his daughter for the first time since 11/88.

The mother denied that the father constantly tried to contact her regarding visiting the children in 8/89. The mother advised, when the father does contact her, he seldom ask about the children.

The mother feels that the father has poor judgment concerning the children. Mother advised, that her husband, in the past, has done things to the children which she felt wasn't appropriate. For example, the mother alleges, that in 7/89, when the father was visiting the children at her home, he referred to her on several occasions as a "bitch." In 11/88, the mother alleges, that the father locked the children in the car to follow her into the store.

Ms. ▮ alleges, that her husband is extremely violent. She reiterated the charges that she made at Family Court Intake against her husband, stating that when she was 5½ months pregnant, he strangled her, causing her to lose one of her twins. She also acknowledged, that she was a "high risk" pregnancy and stated, that her husband's constant physical abuse towards her, helped to worsen the situation.

The mother also advised, that she was in fact, working against the doctor's orders but only, because her husband complained about the loss of income that would have existed.

The mother also alleges, that she has never been the aggressor in any of their confrontations; The mother stated that she did in fact, fight her husband on 7/10/89, but only after he had assaulted her several times and seemed as though he wasn't going to stop.

The mother advised that in 8/88, she left her husband; After a few weeks, mother alleges, that the father apologized and promised not to hit her again. A few days after her return, mother alleges, father picked her up and threw her to the ground, causing torn ligaments.

Fig. 2 - cont'd

CASE #647625   OFFICER: SNELLA

In 9/88, mother left the father again, allegedly returning in 10/88,
to get her belongings; Mother stated, the father is lying regarding
his allegation that he asked her to leave. To this date, the mother
stated that she has no intention of returning to the father's home.

OFFICER'S NOTES:

The mother and her two children are residing with the MGM, ███████████,
in a three bedroom apartment. Children ██████ and ████████ each have
their own bed and their room was found to be adequate and clean.

Officer has made several attempts to contact the father but has not
been able to reach him.

W: 12/15/89

T: 12/15/89

Fig. 2 - cont'd

At a Term of the Family Court of
the State of New York, held in and
for the County of New York

at **60 LaFayette St.**

on **12/18/54**

PRESENT:

HON: **R. J. Zuckerman**
    JUDGE

IN THE MATTER OF

▆▆▆▆▆▆▆▆▆▆▆▆
Petitioner

vs   Docket No: ▆▆▆▆▆▆

Lettie Ivette ▆▆▆▆   All Purpose Short Order
Respondent

· On the consent of the parties, the petitioner father shall have visitation with the children ▆▆▆▆▆ (d.o.b. ▆▆ and ▆▆▆▆▆▆ (d.o.b. ▆▆) as follows:

1) Upon 7 days advance notice, the father may have visitation Saturday 12pm until Sunday 7pm.

2) Father agrees to pick up children from respondent's home at the start of visitation and return the children to respondent's home at the close of visitation.

3) All overnight visitation is to take place at the home of the paternal grandmother, ▆▆▆▆▆   ENTER:

▆▆▆▆▆▆▆▆

Judge of the Family Court
Ruth Jane Zuckerman

Fig. 3 Despite repeated mentions of abuse, the judge made my children and myself virtual prisoners of New York

At a Term of the Family Court of
the State of New York, held in and
for the County of New York

at _60 LaFayette st._

on _12/18/89_

PRESENT:

HON: _R. J. Zuckerman_
          JUDGE

IN THE MATTER OF

Petitioner ▓▓▓▓▓▓

                vs   Docket No. ▓▓▓▓▓▓

Lettie Ivette ▓▓▓▓▓▓   All Purpose Short Order.
Respondent

----

4) The father is to obtain a crib for
the child ▓▓▓ prior to overnight visitation
taking place.

5) NY SPCC is to visit the paternal grandmother
home to ascertain whether it is adequate for
overnight visitation. NY SPCC may recalendar this
matter if the paternal grandmother's home is
inappropriate for overnight visitation.

6) Neither party is to move the permanent residence
of the children out of the Jurisdiction

7) The parties are encouraged to arrange
additional visitation when the father is
available.

ENTER:

[signature]

Judge of the Family Court

RUTH JANE ZUCKERMAN

Fig. 3 cont'd

Department of the Army
Alpha Company, 50th Signal Battalion (Corps)
(Command Operations) (Airborne)
Fort Bragg, North Carolina, 28307-5000

AFZA-AS-SB-AA

MEMORANDUM FOR: NEW YORK CITY COURT SYSTEM

SUBJECT: PERSONAL CONDUCT OF SSG ▓▓▓▓▓, ▓▓▓▓, ▓▓▓▓▓, ▓▓▓▓▓▓
BRIGADE, FORT BRAGG, NORTH CAROLINA 28307-5000

TO: WHOM IT MAY CONCERN.

1. I have been assigned to HHC, 35TH Signal Brigade since 1 February 1988 and
performed as the unit First Sergeant from April until August 1989. I have known
SSG ▓▓▓▓▓ for most of that time, and worked very closely with him during my
First Sergeant's tour. He was the Platoon Sergeant for the Brigade's Automation
Section. I submit the following support information for SSG ▓▓▓▓▓ on my own
free will and accord, because I truely belive that the Soldier's spouse is intentionally trying to cause undue harassment upon the Soldier.

2. I was briefed on the situation of Sergeant ▓▓▓▓▓ by my predecessor (1SG
Paul Miller). He had already concluded the same opinion that I later concluded.
I personally checked the support arrangements made by Sergeant ▓▓▓▓▓ for his
family, Everything was in order according to the XVIII Airborne Corps Legal Assistance
Office.

3. When I assumed the position of First Sergeant, the Company Commander was in the
process of answering a Command Level Complaint made by Mrs. ▓▓▓▓▓ reguarding
the non receipt of support money from her husband. After thoroughly investigating
this matter, it was learned that Mrs. ▓▓▓▓▓ was not picking up her mail. This
fact was further substantiated by the return of a letter from the Company Commander
to Mrs. ▓▓▓▓▓ as being not deliverable. After investigation, each complaint
made by Mrs. ▓▓▓▓▓ to this Command has been determinded to be unfounded.

4. I further submit that SSG ▓▓▓▓▓ competence and personal commitment to
to excellence is unquestionable. During my tour as his First Sergeant, we had
numerous consultations reguarding his family situation, and he never implied any
short cuts reguarding their support or well being. SSG ▓▓▓▓▓ is a strong,
professional NCO. His loyalty, devotion to duty, selfless service, and support
to me as his First Sergeant was significant to my success. Therefore, with all
things considered, I have concluded that Mrs. ▓▓▓▓▓ is intentionally trying
to cause her husband undue harassment, in any way that she can.

AL F. McKOY
SGM, USA
HHC, 35TH SIGNAL BRIGADE

*Fig. 4 I found this letter in my family court file almost twenty years later. It explains why
the courts never believed me about the abuse.*

Only Victor's name appeared on my daughter's headstone.

Chapter 14

Winter 1988 — Her Last Breath

I was terrified by the time I arrived in the delivery room. No one was there to hold my hand, or to tell me everything was going to be okay. Doctors and nurses ran around the delivery room and failed miserably at trying to calm me down. I was too busy screaming from the pain and crying for the doctors to stop my labor.

The doctor yelled at the nurses, "Find a vein and get an IV line going NOW!"

I felt a shot of pain in my arms from where the nurses were hitting me as they desperately tried to get a vein to pop up.

"Doctor, all her veins have collapsed!" I heard a nurse say.

Someone exclaimed, "I got one!"

Someone else yelled, "Get it, get it, get it!"

Then the doctor walked over to me.

"We're going to have to deliver those babies now. They're in distress and it's too late to stop your labor."

Through my tears, I yelled with all the strength I had.

"You can't take them now! It's not time!"

"We have to. If we don't deliver them now, all of you are going to die," the doctor said.

My thoughts ran back to earlier in the day when Victor strangled me and I couldn't breathe. The stress of fighting, along with the lack of oxygen, put my babies in distress. The doctor left my side and went to the foot of the bed while the nurses secured my feet in the stirrups. Everything happened so fast and the labor pains were so intense; it felt as if someone stuck hot knives into my belly. Then my thoughts turned elsewhere. Was this God's punishment? What did I do wrong to deserve this? I was raised to believe that God had two faces; one that was loving and forgiving and the other one was mean and punished those who disobeyed him. All I did was marry a man because I loved him! What was so wrong about that?

The doctor broke my train of thought as he examined me to see how much more I had dilated.

"Don't push!" The doctor yelled at me while he continues his examination.

"I'm not pushing!" I yelled back.

I tried to close my legs a little but couldn't because of the stirrups. I wanted to resist the urge to push but I could feel a baby trying to come out anyway. The doctor bent down in front of me to prepare to deliver the first baby. He turned his head to say something to the nurse when, all of a sudden, he screamed, "OH SHIT!"

When he stood up, he held my baby upside down by her feet and his hospital gown was completely splattered with blood. The baby had to have come out feet first because of how he grabbed it. When the doctor yelled, I lifted my head off the bed and strained to see her. She was so tiny and I didn't even hear her cry. I just saw the baby's back as the doctor handed it to the nurse, who quickly ran out of the delivery room with her. Right away, I felt dizzy.

"The other baby's transverse!" I heard a nurse say.

When an unborn baby is in a transverse position, it lays across the mother's pelvic bone instead of the normal birth position of head down. It was dangerous for me as well as for my baby, because there was a possibility that my uterus could have ruptured which could have lead to both of our deaths.

The nurse grabbed my belly tightly where the still unborn twin was, trying to keep the baby from moving any further. The pain was excruciating. As the doctor moved back to the side of my bed, he told me what he had to do.

"Ivette, I have to give you an emergency cesarean section. The anesthesiologist has been called and he's on his way here."

I didn't want to die like this! What would happen to my children? With the remaining strength I had, I motioned for a nurse to come to me.

"I need you to call my Kingdom Hall and ask for the pastor. Tell him it's an emergency and I need him here now!"

I looked at the clock on the wall and it was close to midnight. I had memorized the number so I gave it to her and she ran off. The other nurse was still holding my stomach and she was hurting me so bad that I tried to push her hand away.

"If we let this baby move, you're both going to die! Ivette, Stop it!" the nurse screamed at me.

I yelled out again what my religion was and that I didn't want a blood transfusion. When I saw the doctor again, I asked how my first baby was.

"So far, you had a girl and we're not sure how she is right now. The ambulance took her to Cape Fear Valley Medical Center where they have a neonatal unit and we have another ambulance on standby waiting to take this baby."

It seemed like an eternity before the pastor finally arrived in the delivery room. Through my tears, I told the pastor what happened.

"Please pray with me. I can't do this alone," I told him.

He held my hands tightly, closed his eyes and I closed mine.

"Lord, we humbly come to you in this time of need to watch over our Sister who needs you now more than ever. Whatever your Will is, Lord, will be. Lord, I ask you to watch over her babies, that they be healthy and safe. In Jesus' name we ask you, Amen."

I said "Amen."

As soon as he finished praying, a peace came over me like I've never experienced before.

I looked at him and said, "Thank you, thank you."

I continued to think about Victoria and how I didn't want her to grow up without a mother.

I said under my breath, "God, this can't be it. But if you want to take me now, I'm ready. If you allow me to survive this, I will know you have bigger plans for me." Then I closed my eyes.

The pastor was quickly ushered out of the delivery room by the nurse as the anesthesiologist entered the room. He walked up to me and told me that he was going to put me under.

I had to say it again. "Whatever happens, please don't give me blood. Even if it means I'm going to die," I whispered to him.

"If that's what you wish," he said calmly.

He put the mask over my nose and mouth and asked me to count backwards from twenty.

"Twenty, nineteen, eighteen, seventeen, sixteen, fifteen…." Then darkness overcame me.

"Ivette, Ivette, wake up," I heard someone say, lightly slapping my face. I felt dizzy, weak and groggy and it took a few minutes to register where I was. I slowly opened my eyes and saw the doctor standing over me. My throat felt dry and I could only speak in a whisper.

"What happened? Are they all right?"

The doctor spoke. "Ivette, you had two girls. They have both been taken to Cape Fear Valley Medical Center to their Neonatal Intensive Care unit. You've lost a large amount of blood and we honored your wishes not to give you a blood transfusion. Ivette, because of the large amount of blood you've lost from the vaginal delivery and from the cesarean, we don't believe you'll make it through the night. Do you have any family down here we can call?"

After everything that happened during the night, I wondered why Victor hadn't come to the hospital while I was in labor. I found out years later from reading medical records that the hospital did call him and he told them he couldn't come.

I lay there and looked at the doctor through half-closed eyes while my mind processed what he just said.

"No, all my family is in New York. Can you please call my mother?"

I realized it was after midnight and knew she would be at work. My sister Bernice was home and my Mom had three-way calling on her phone. Bernice would make sure to connect the call to my mother at work.

"We can't make long-distance calls here," the doctor said. I couldn't believe what I was hearing; first the doctor tells me I'm going to die then tells me he can't make long-distance calls?

I mustered up enough strength to yell. "Call my parents!"

He asked the nurse to get a pen and piece of paper for me and I wrote down the number. He then took the paper from the nurse and went to dial the phone that was in the delivery room.

I heard the phone ring and my sister answer the phone. Then I heard the doctor talking.

"This is Doctor Marcus from Fort Bragg Hospital in North Carolina. Who am I speaking to?"

I could hear my sister's voice. The doctor told my sister what my condition was.

"Someone needs to hurry up and get down here. She's delivered the twins and lost a lot of blood during the deliveries and we believe she won't survive through the night. There's nothing else we can do for her," I heard the doctor tell my sister.

The doctor gave the phone to me. I could barely talk above a whisper.

"Bernice, call Mommy and Daddy."

She told me to hold on, called my Mom at work and made a three-way call. I heard Bernice repeat to my parents what the doctor told her. Then she connected my father who had moved out when I was about sixteen. Once I heard both my parents, I started crying.

"Mommy? Daddy? I'm in the delivery room. I had the twins. It was all Victor's fault." I couldn't stop crying.

"We'll be right down there. We're on our way," my mother said

I gave the phone back to the doctor and thanked him.

I hadn't made it out of the delivery room before the phone rang. One of the nurses brought the phone over to me.

"Mrs. Ivette Wilson?" I heard.

"Yes?" I responded.

"This is the doctor at Cape Fear Valley Medical Center. We have your daughters. They are in bad shape and need a blood transfusion."

I feared the worst, but I had to hold true to my religious beliefs. Jehovah's Witnesses were taught that ingesting blood, even in a medical emergency, was against God's law and therefore would warrant excommunication.

"I do not want them to have blood," stating again, what my religion was. Then the doctor cut me off in mid-sentence.

"Without a blood transfusion, they'll die," he said. Although I was still weak from the surgery, I mustered all the strength I had to respond to him.

"You can't guarantee that my babies will live if you give them blood." Once again, I stated my religion.

"I didn't accept blood for myself. It's in God's hands now." The doctor sounded as if he was getting agitated with me.

"Then we have no other choice but to go to court and get an injunction against you to give these babies a life-saving blood transfusion."

I couldn't believe what I was hearing! Before I could respond to the doctor, I heard a click.

I was still on the gurney on my back with tears streaming down my face. I felt so helpless and thought that all of this was my fault and, even worse, I was in no condition to help my babies or to be there for them. If I had left Victor sooner, this wouldn't have happened. I'd have two healthy twin girls that I could watch grow up. Now I might not have either of them. As I was pushed out of the delivery room, I said a silent prayer for my girls.

I woke up the next morning in a room with three other women on the maternity ward. The other women had their babies with them, cuddling them, kissing them and their families fawned over their newest addition. I felt sad that I didn't have my babies with me and I was still in a lot of pain from the surgery. All I could think about was whether my babies were going to be okay and I knew if I were there, they wouldn't feel alone. I felt like I was being ripped apart slowly, limb by limb just watching the other mothers interact with their babies. Minutes later, a nurse arrived by my bedside carrying Victoria. It looked like she had been crying too. I was so happy to see her that I couldn't stop hugging and kissing her. The nurse laid her in the bed with me before taking my pulse. Victoria hugged me so hard she choked me.

"How are you feeling, Ivette?" the nurse said.

"Like crap," I whispered.

My belly still hurt from the staples they put in me after the C-section.

"How are my babies?" The nurse told me she didn't know. Then she came over and touched my arm.

"We're going to move you to the female surgery ward as soon as a bed is available," she said. I was glad for that because with the other babies crying, my breasts started leaking. I asked the nurse for another gown. She noticed that and got a gown for me.

"We're going to give you something for your pain and something to dry up the milk," she said. I grew even more concerned because something didn't feel right. I didn't want anything to dry up my breast milk; I wanted to breastfeed my girls! But there was no one at the hospital that could take the breast milk to Cape Fear for my daughters. My parents hadn't gotten there yet and I was just glad to have Victoria next to me. She stuck to me like glue and wouldn't let the nurse take my temperature in peace.

I managed to close my eyes for a bit to rest and process everything that transpired the night before. Victoria soon stopped moving and fell asleep. Poor baby. I knew she was exhausted because this was rough on her too. Then Victor woke me up by calling out to me. When I opened my eyes, the first thing I noticed was a bag in his hand and I knew that type of bag well; it meant he bought vinyl records from the store. When he looked at me, I turned my head away from him. I had a sinking feeling in the pit of my stomach that he had bad news.

"I just came from Cape Fear," he said.

He had papers in his hand and he put them on my lap. By then Victoria woke up. He tried reaching for her, but she had a crying fit and tried to scoot away from him. She was only eight-months old and hadn't started walking, so I tried to keep her still so she wouldn't crawl on my stomach.

"You have to sign the girls' birth certificates." I picked them up and looked at them. One was for Susan Michelle* and the other one was for Yolanda Nadia Wilson.* Victor was silent while I signed the birth certificates in the space reserved for the mother. I couldn't even bring myself to talk to him and I wanted him out of my room. I couldn't believe he named one of MY daughters after his mother and didn't even ask me! Using one of MY children to honor his lying ass mother!

"Susan Michelle died this morning," he said.

I looked up at him. The tears welled up in my eyes and I started to cough. Then Victor told me about the conversation he had with the doctor that hung up on me, and he gave his consent to the hospital to give the twins a blood transfusion. Then he told me that his mother sent him money to take care of Little Susan's funeral.

With my free arm, I grabbed a pillow and put it over my belly to keep the incision from tearing. Then cried hysterically. Victor acted as if he couldn't see that I was upset and talked to me with a sad puppy-dog look on his face.

"Yolanda is still not out of the woods, though. The Military Police are waiting outside to talk to you about what happened. Look, Susan Michelle is already dead. It doesn't make sense for you to get me in trouble with the MPs by telling them anything. It won't bring her back."

What nerve! I just stared at him. The day before, he looked confident when he told the MPs he didn't lay a hand on me. This time, he looked scared. Just as he walked out, two MPs came into my room.

"Remember what I said," he responded.

I didn't say a word to him as he walked past the MPs out of my room.

"Ivette, we heard about what happened and we're sorry for your loss," one of the officers began.

I was still crying and tried to catch my breath.

"Thank you," I said before the officer continued.

"Ma'am, we're here to let you know that we are ready to arrest your husband for attempted murder for you and manslaughter for the death of your daughter and we would like to get a statement from you."

I didn't know what manslaughter meant at the time, nor did I care. I only knew what happened to me. At that moment, I was faced with the most difficult decision I've ever had to make in my life. Do I press charges against Victor and see him court marshaled and go to jail? That could take months. Where would I live in the meantime? Did I want to stay in North Carolina? How was I going to support the girls and myself? The doctor knew what happened but no one offered me any help; not even a safe place to stay. Victor had already taken so much from me already; my dignity, my self-respect, years of my life and, most importantly, my precious daughter. I finally made my decision and my decision was to leave it in God's hands.

"I'm not going to press charges." The MPs just looked at each other, completely baffled.

"This man has taken everything from me and he's gotten away with all of it. When I called the MPs the day before, they didn't believe me — they just left me there with him. Whenever I told someone about his abuse — his commanding officer, other MPs, NO ONE believed me. He even told people that I was emotionally unstable just to discredit me. He's gotten away with it before and he'll get away with it this time. No officers, I don't want to press charges. I have total faith in God and I'm going to leave this in God's hands. God will make sure that he gets exactly what he deserves."

For a few seconds, the officers were speechless. They tried again to convince me to press charges against Victor, but I cut them off in mid-sentence.

"I've already lost one daughter and I wasn't there for her. I could lose the other one now. I do not want to spend any more time mixed up with Victor so I can't be there for my other daughter." That was the end of the conversation and the MPs left my room.

Shortly after they left, my parents came into my room. Victoria's eyes lit up as her grandma and grandpa came into the room. I was teary-eyed, still grieving for my lost daughter. My mom had a very forlorn look on her face as she tried to hold back the tears. The moment my father saw me, he started to cry. "Vettie" was all he could say. I asked what took them so long to get to North Carolina. My father told me he was so upset that he stayed on the plane instead of getting off in North Carolina. They came over to my bed and they both kissed me. I asked them if they saw Victor on the way in.

My mother put her hands on her hips and started shaking her head. That meant she was getting riled up.

"Victor knows better than to let me see him at this point!" My mother said.

I was never more confused in my life then at that moment, because one minute my mother would defend Victor, the next minute she wanted to strangle him. While my parents talked to each other and Victoria, I turned my head towards the window and stared off into space.

I wanted to go to Cape Fear to see my twins and I was desperately worried about Yolanda and whether I would lose her too. I felt guilty, helpless and depressed that I wasn't there for Little Susan. I always felt that if Little Susan knew I was there, that if I had been able to touch her, it would have given her the strength to live. It is every mother's right to hold her child and bond with it at birth and Victor robbed me of that. The doctors and nurses checked on me frequently, checking my temperature and pulse because that was all they could do for me. Doctor Marcus commented that he was surprised that I had made it that far because I didn't have a blood transfusion and the only thing they could do was give me oxygen. But I knew that my faith in God had carried me all this way and He wasn't about to let me down now.

I was stuck in that stupid military hospital on Fort Bragg, thinking that with all the billions of dollars the military spends, they couldn't spend the money on a decent neonatal unit so my babies wouldn't be fifteen miles away from me in another hospital. Mentally, I was drained. Physically I was drained. I couldn't get out of bed because I still felt very dizzy from the blood loss and my incision hurt. My parents were still in my room when I asked them if they could make the funeral arrangements and pick out something for Little Susan to be buried in. When Doctor Marcus came into the room and I introduced him to my parents, he informed me that they were preparing for me to attend little Susan's wake and funeral the next day, March 5. Everyone on the ward heard about what happened to the twins and me and I felt like they were walking on eggshells around me. As usual, I wasn't surprised that I didn't receive a phone call from his mother asking how I was and after Victor left, he didn't come back to the hospital. Because he was such a sympathy-seeker, I assumed he had concocted a story to tell people so they could feel sorry for him.

My parents agreed to get something for little Susan to wear and took Victoria back to the townhouse on base so I could get some rest. I wondered what it was like with my parents and Victor under the same roof as I drifted off to sleep.

I woke up the next morning feeling tired, as if I hadn't slept at all. So much had happened in the past couple of days and I wasn't sure if I could handle all of the stress of going to the funeral home and the hospital in the same day. When one of the nurses came to my room to help me get washed up and dressed, I took my time so I could prepare myself mentally to go to my daughter's funeral. Thank goodness the hospital provided me with a wheel chair because I was too weak to stand, let alone walk.

The next thing I remember was being at the funeral home. I don't remember leaving the hospital, or driving to the funeral home. It was like a dream where one scene jumps to another. My mother wheeled me into the funeral home with my father walking behind us while he held Victoria. I didn't notice how many people were there because all of my attention was focused on the small, white, satin-covered casket at the front of the room. I couldn't take my eyes off of it because it was so tiny and at no more than twenty-four inches, I had never seen anything like it. As my mother pushed me closer and closer to Little Susan's casket, I felt sick to my stomach from the unbearable grief and pain. I finally reached my baby's casket and my parents each grabbed one of my arms to help me out of the wheelchair so I could walk the last few steps towards Little Susan. The lid was open and there was a small, white stuffed lamb in her casket, a gift from one of my older half-sisters. While I stood there and stared at her, my legs started to shake. Nothing in this world could have prepared me for what I was looking at. She was so beautiful and tiny, being born at twenty-six weeks and only two and a half pounds. She was light-skinned, had a head full of dark hair and wore a little white dress with a bonnet that was too big for her. I touched the few strands of hair that peeked out from under her bonnet. Then I let out a horrible moan. It hurt so bad to see my child like this. It wasn't supposed to be like this! I thought.

"My poor little girl, my poor little girl, my baby," I said aloud while tears streamed down my face.

When I looked at her, I could tell that she was fighting to live and her tiny, fragile body took a beating in the process. Her skin was so thin and transparent that I saw the veins in her little arms and face. When she passed away and the hospital removed her from the ventilator, the tape on her upper lip removed some of her delicate skin, which left a red mark. The IV lines that helped to keep her alive left black and blue bruises on her fragile arms and legs.

Holding onto the side of the railing where her casket laid, I reached out stroked her little hands and was startled at how cold they were. My mother's instinct kicked in as I had an overwhelming urge to pick her up and cradle her, to let her know I was there, but I knew I couldn't do that. I cared about nothing or no one else but my child laying there before me, cold and motionless. I stood there, talked to her and cried. My chest was so tight that I could hardly breathe.

"Mommy's so very sorry. I didn't want this to happen to you. You didn't deserve this."

My mother must have sensed that I was about to collapse when she patted me on my back.

"It's time to go now."

I knew we had to leave to go to the cemetery for her burial.

I told my mother, "I'm not leaving my baby. I wasn't there for her while she fought for her life, but I'm going to be here for her now."

I wanted to stay there and look at my baby and have her image burned into my memory forever because once I left, I knew I would never see her again. I wanted Little Susan to have something of mine so she would always know her mother loved her and would always be with her. So, when I leaned over and kissed her forehead, tears streamed down my face and fell into her casket, on her face and dress. As I stood up, my mother gently guided me back into the wheelchair and I sat down. The hardest part was yet to come.

Chapter 15

Winter 1988 — Saying Goodbye and Hello

I was so consumed by grief that although the drive to the cemetery was a blur, I remembered it was cold and rainy outside. As the rain hit the car's windshield, I thought to myself that this was God's way of grieving with me for my daughter. My face was still red and swollen from crying at the funeral home and the only thing I saw in my mind's eye was my baby girl in her casket. For as long as I live, I will NEVER get that vision out of my head. I was beaten down emotionally and psychologically and still had to go the hospital to see Yolanda. When we finally arrived at the cemetery on Fort Bragg, I didn't want to get out of the car because I didn't want to say goodbye to Little Susan. Although still weak from giving birth, I had to walk to where the service was being held because the wheelchair couldn't move over the wet grass and mud. Once we got to the tent, I was able to sit in the wheelchair while my father pushed me in. The pastor from the Kingdom Hall that came to the hospital and prayed with me was there to conduct Little Susan's funeral service and that gave me comfort. I saw my daughter's little white casket, this time, at the front of the tent and it was closed. I wanted to open it again to say goodbye, but thought better of it. As my father pushed me closer to the casket to say my final goodbye to my precious little girl, my mother held Victoria and tried to keep her quiet. When Victor approached my mother to take Victoria from her, she cried and squirmed away from him and wrapped her arms around my mother's neck. As I looked at Little Susan's casket, the pain was overwhelming.

"Mommy's so sorry," I said aloud while shaking my head.

My father pulled back my wheelchair and pushed me towards the end of the first row of chairs where my mother sat with Victoria. As the pastor began the service with a prayer, I noticed that Victor came and sat next to me, which was the first time I saw him since he told me Little Susan died. After the pastor finished saying the prayer and everyone said "Amen," he began the service. Tears streamed down my face when Victor put his arm around me and patted my shoulder, as if everything was going to be all right. Right then and there, with all the strength I had, I took his arm and threw it off me and shoved him so hard he almost fell out of his seat. That's when I couldn't contain my anger anymore.

"Don't you DARE touch me! YOU'RE THE REASON WHY SHE'S HERE!"

Obviously embarrassed, Victor got up without saying a word, moved away from me, and sat next to someone else. I didn't care who stared at me or thought I was crazy because I briefly disrupted my own daughter's funeral service. I could have sworn I heard Victor say to someone, "I think she's losing her mind."

Years later I found out that Victor told people at his job the story of how Little Susan died in his arms just to get people to feel sorry for him. After getting up enough nerve to talk to the doctors that took care of Little Susan almost a year later, they told me that by the time Victor held her, she had already died. Not even a heart or lung transplant would have helped her because her heart and lungs weren't developed enough. I even heard that people at his job collected money for him and put it in a card and his supervisors gave him a few days off. Victor never told me any of this. As long as he was able to play on people's sympathy, no one would ever believe that such an upstanding service member could be capable of assaulting his wife and causing the death of his own child.

My mother held Victoria while she tried to calm me down at the same time. The service was about to be over, and soon it would be time to go to the hospital to see Yolanda. As cheap as Victor was and as much as he made fun of my religion and my beliefs, he was happy that he didn't have to pay for the funeral or burial because Little Susan was the dependent of an active duty service member.

That day, it seemed everything moved in slow motion. After the funeral was over, we went to Cape Fear Valley Medical Center to see Yolanda. When we made it to the neonatal intensive care unit, my father pushed my wheelchair up to the nurses' station. I mentioned to one of the nurses who I was and that I wanted to see my daughter. The nurse I spoke to was the nurse who took care of Yolanda. She got up from her desk, walked towards me and asked us to follow her. Just as we got to the doors of the neonatal intensive care unit, the nurse stopped and turned towards me.

"We're so sorry for your loss and we thought you would want this," she said.

The nurse handed me several Polaroid pictures of Little Susan and Yolanda. Seeing those pictures was like pouring salt on a fresh wound. There were pictures of Little Susan while she was alive, hooked up to all sorts of tubes and wires and a couple of pictures of her after she died in addition to an imprint of her tiny feet on a piece of paper. In one of the pictures of Little Susan after she passed away, someone's hand was gently holding her head up. My baby was so tiny that the hand was much larger than her head. Then there were a few pictures of Yolanda, hooked up to all sorts of wires and tubes as well. I just stared at the pictures and felt a sharp pain in my chest. While I was so grateful for this, it ripped my soul apart to know that my babies were in pain from being handled by people other than me and stuck with needles. Before we went through the doors into the unit, the nurse cautioned me.

"I want to remind you to just focus on Yolanda and not the other children here. Spend some time with her and let her know you're here." I nodded my head.

As my parents wheeled me toward Yolanda's incubator, I couldn't help but notice the other babies in the unit. There was a baby right next to Yolanda who was smaller than she was and I asked the nurse about that baby. She told me the baby was only one and a half pounds and the mother gave birth to her at eight months. Premature babies suffer from apnea, which is a period where the baby stops breathing. Because she was so tiny, her bed automatically rocked back and forth to keep her heart from stopping.

As painful as it was to see another mother going through what I was going through, I tried to re-focus my attention on Yolanda. She was hooked up to a heart monitor, had tubes in her tiny chest to remove any fluid buildup, IVs for medication and even a valve was inserted in her ankle so the nurse could turn turned the knob to get blood samples. She also had a feeding tube in her mouth as well because she had no sucking reflex. Whatever was left of my heart after Little Susan died just crumbled when I saw Yolanda. She was equally as beautiful and her complexion was slightly darker than Little Susan, but with the same head full of gorgeous dark hair. She sounded like a mouse when she opened her mouth to cry. I took a deep breath as my parents helped me stand up so I could put on a hospital gown and wash my hands. Because she was so small, I wasn't allowed to pick her up, so I had to reach into the incubator to touch her. When I rubbed her little hands and arms, her heart rate increased — she knew I was there! I cried and said a silent prayer to God to spare Yolanda's life because I knew I couldn't survive losing my other twin. I sat Victoria on my lap so she could see and touch Yolanda too.

"Baby," I said to Victoria.

Although Victoria was only eight months old, she caught on quickly as she repeated the word.

"Baby," she said. Then she smiled, showing off all four of her teeth.

I came to the realization that although I was supposed to have three daughters, maybe God knew I couldn't handle three babies. I got angry all over again because Victor's actions cheated me out of the precious opportunity to see and hold Little Susan and Yolanda and to bond with them. All of this happened because Victor was selfish, didn't want three kids and I wouldn't get an abortion. I asked the nurse why I couldn't pick Yolanda up and she cautioned me that at only two and a half pounds, holding her would have caused her to burn more calories and she couldn't afford to lose any weight. I stared at Yolanda while thinking about Little Susan. I held Victoria, stroked Yolanda's hair and rubbed her arms and legs. I even let Victoria put her hand in the incubator to touch her little sister.

I was so drained from the day's events that I couldn't stay at the hospital too long but I didn't want to leave Yolanda alone in the hospital. My mother took Victoria from me as my father helped me back into the wheelchair. I reached into Yolanda's incubator and said goodbye.

"Mommy's here now, just hang in there. I'll be back soon."

Having to say goodbye to one child and hello to another all in one day had a profound effect on me that will last until I draw my last breath. Although I spent fourteen days in the hospital, I was glad to be away from Victor. My dad had to go back to New York and my mother stayed behind in North Carolina to help take care of Victoria. None of Victor's co-workers or friends came or even called the hospital to see how I was, just like when Victoria was born. I don't know why I expected them to, but I did. I was grateful that my mom brought Victoria to see me every day so I could spend some time with her.

I used the time I spent in the hospital to my advantage to figure out a way to take my girls and leave Victor without any of us getting hurt. I couldn't leave until Yolanda was out of the hospital and that wouldn't be for at least another three months. I had three more months of hell with this man and three more months to plan my exit. Victor had already threatened several times what would happen to me if I left and I had no doubts that he would keep his word. First things first. Yolanda had to be well enough to leave the hospital.

Soon, I was well enough to be discharged from the hospital. Although I didn't want to be in the house with Victor, I didn't know about other options, such as a shelter. Even if I did go to a shelter, Victor would find us. Nonetheless, I was happy to be at home with Victoria. Victor knew he had to tread lightly around my mother, so he made sure to keep himself out of my mother's eyesight as long as she was there. It was difficult for me to go upstairs to the same bedroom where weeks earlier, Victor strangled me. I tried to occupy myself with taking care of Victoria and spending time at the hospital with Yolanda. I tried to see her as much as I could before my mother left, because Victor would soon be up to his old tricks again. To make matters worse, he never gave me back the other set of car keys so I could continue to go to the hospital to see Yolanda. His sportier "club" car sat in front of the house while he drove the other car to work.

"You don't have money to put gas in the car," I heard. Or, "I need it later. I'm going out tonight." With everything that happened so far, I half-expected Victor to change his behavior, but yet again, he proved to me that he would never change.

Some members of the Kingdom Hall heard about what happened and came by my house to see me. Occasionally, they would offer to watch Victoria or drive me to the hospital to see Yolanda, but I knew I couldn't rely on them forever. One day, some women from my Kingdom Hall came by to visit. They sat in the living room and were talking to me when Victor came home. They respectfully said hello to him and he just stared at them and gave them dirty looks until they felt so uncomfortable they said they had to leave. He literally kept me isolated by chasing away anyone that I tried to be friends with or showed any concern for me. Because I had no transportation, I was only able to get to the hospital to see Yolanda two or three times a week and that was through the kindness and generosity of other people.

Although I tried not to speak to Victor, he tried talking to me as if nothing happened. It had been about a month since Little Susan died and I wanted to go to the cemetery to visit her grave. I asked Victor for the death certificate so I could see where she was buried.

"Why do you need it?" he said.

"I want to know where my daughter is buried," I replied. Victor gave me a matter-of-fact look.

"These papers are mine. I paid for her birth certificate and death certificate. If you want to know where she's buried, go and pay for your own copy of her death certificate."

I rolled my eyes, sighed and went upstairs to get Victoria dressed, determined to find my daughter's grave. I grabbed my coat, put Victoria in her stroller and walked to the cemetery, which took me about an hour. It was quite a walk, but I needed it to try to clear my head. When Victoria and I finally arrived at the cemetery, I tried to remember my surroundings from the day of her funeral to find her grave. After some walking, I finally found it. I thought I would find some peace spending time there, but once again, I got a cold hard slap in the face. Her headstone read:

Susan Michelle Wilson

March 3 – March 4, 1988

Beloved daughter of Sgt. Victor Wilson

My name was nowhere on the headstone! It was bad enough that I lost my daughter in such a horrible way and that I could still lose her sister. But to see just Victor's name on Little Susan's headstone was like a hot knife going through butter. I looked around at the other tombstones to see if that was the norm and it wasn't. There were headstones of other children that had both parent's names. My God! I thought. How far would this man go? Like he gave birth to her! She was MY daughter too! I almost died giving birth to her! I felt as if I had been punched in the stomach. I stood at my daughter's grave and through my tears, silently vowed that no matter how long it took, I would not let her death be in vain.

I stayed at Little Susan's grave with Victoria for a little while longer before we started on our way back home. I just couldn't wrap my head around this one. When Little Susan died, all I got was "I'm sorry for your loss." There was no one for me to talk to who really understood what I was going through — the violence, the abuse, the loss of my daughter or coping with taking care of two babies. So many emotions were trapped inside of me with no way of letting them out, that I felt like a prisoner living on Fort Bragg. Even worse, a prisoner with a target on her back. Victor had gotten away with everything he had ever done to me, so there was no reason for me to ever believe that either my children or me would ever get justice. I had to resign myself to leaving it in God's hands. When Victoria and I finally got home, Victor was home as well. I neither looked at him nor tried not to talk to him and was glad that he said nothing to me. I was still in pain from my surgery, was tired all the time and walking to the cemetery didn't help. I carried Victoria upstairs and changed her clothes for bed. Not long after, I heard Victor's footsteps on the stairs. He went into the bathroom then I heard water running. I sighed deeply. Thank God, he's not coming into the bedroom I thought to myself. In an attempt to calm down, I turned on the TV and lay down with Victoria. Minutes later, Victor came out of the bathroom and into the bedroom with a towel wrapped around his waist. When he got closer to me, Victoria sat up and started crying.

"Why is she crying?" he asked as he took off his towel.

I was shocked that he had the nerve to walk in front of Victoria with nothing on.

"Victor, I've told you several times not to walk around Victoria with nothing on! Put a towel around yourself!"

I couldn't get Victoria to stop crying and her face was turning red. Victor stood there and stared at her.

Then he grabbed his crotch and laughed.

"I've got something to shut her up!"

I was mortified that he would make a sexual innuendo to his own child! This was his own flesh and blood he was saying this to! I grabbed Victoria, ran into her room, and slammed the door. Damn, I've got to hurry up and get out of here! If he was abusive to me, it would just be a matter of time before this sick individual started abusing my daughters!

Every time Victor agitated Victoria, it always took me a while to calm her down. After an hour or so of rocking her and singing to her, I was able to get her calmed down enough for her to go to sleep. It wasn't long afterwards that I joined her.

Chapter 16

Spring 1988 — Taking What He Wanted

After I woke up from my nap, I took the opportunity to take a quick shower, so I grabbed my robe and towel and walked out of her room towards the bathroom. She felt me get up and started crying again, and I didn't want to leave her alone with Victor, so I took her in the bathroom with me. By then, my staples had been removed and there were Steri-Strips covering the staple holes. The doctors warned me to keep that area dry, so I covered the area with a towel whenever I took a shower. When I was done in the shower, I wrapped a towel around me, put my robe on over the towel, picked up Victoria and went back into her room. As soon as I put her down, she started crying again.

"Mommy's going to be back in a minute," I said to her as I left her room.

I felt panicky and anxious as I walked into the bedroom and saw Victor sitting on the bed watching TV. I walked past him as if he wasn't there and went towards the dresser to get some clean underwear and a change of clothes. As I walked past Victor back out of the bedroom, he grabbed me by the arm.

"You know, I could rape you right now and you wouldn't be able to do a fucking thing about it because it's not against the law to rape your wife."

I found out much later that he was right. In 1988, North Carolina's rape law stated that "a person may not be prosecuted under this article if the victim is the person's legal spouse at the time of the commission of the alleged rape or sexual offense, unless the parties are living separate and apart." This law was changed in 1993 to make it a criminal offense to rape your wife.

My heart raced. Victor once told me I didn't have the right to say "No" because I was his wife and he could have sex with me whenever he wanted. I hadn't had sex with Victor since I got pregnant with the twins and I definitely didn't want him touching me now, especially since I knew he was sleeping around and he had a habit of not wearing protection.

"Let me go!" I screamed at him. God please, not now! I thought.

I heard Victoria in the other bedroom crying even louder. I tried to tear my arm away from him, but it was no use. He and I struggled as he tried to take the towel off me and I tried to keep it on. Victor used all his strength to snatch the towel off me, leaving my robe on. Then he got on top of me and raped me, panting and sweating. He didn't care that he was hurting me, or that the stitches in my uterus hadn't completely healed yet from the Cesarean section. As he bounced up and down on top of me, I turned my head to the side and lay there motionless. I stared off into space, trying to forget where I was and praying for him to hurry up and finish. Within minutes, he was done. He said nothing the whole time. He got off of me, picked up the towel and threw it at me as if looking at me suddenly disgusted him, walked out of the bedroom and down the stairs. When I tried to get up, I felt a searing pain in my belly. I put my hand on my belly and as I sat up and looked down at my hand, I saw blood seeping from my unhealed scar. I ran into the bathroom when the nausea overcame me and I vomited violently. When I was done, I cleaned myself, cleaned my stitches and went into Victoria's room, where she was still crying. I didn't bother to go to the hospital to have myself checked out because no one would believe that he actually raped me anyway. All I could do was try to put the rape out of my mind and focus on positive things.

In order to cope with living under the same roof as Victor, I occupied myself with Victoria and called the hospital to check on Yolanda when I had no transportation. Just when I believed I was doing better, the panic attacks started. Whenever Victor came home from work and I heard the sound of the car in front of the house, my heart would beat wildly in my chest, I wouldn't be able to catch my breath and I would sweat and shake uncontrollably. If he didn't come upstairs and I felt I was no longer in danger, the symptoms from the panic attacks would subside.

Days turned into weeks, weeks turned into months. The emotional roller-coaster of Yolanda's condition was a nightmare. The hospital staff would tell me "Yolanda's doing fine today," or "Yolanda lost a few ounces today," or "We took out the chest tubes — she's breathing on her own now," or "We had to put the chest tubes back in — she had trouble breathing." Happy one day that she was breathing on her own, nervous and scared the next day when she wasn't. Her tiny body could only take so much! And, to make matters worse, I still couldn't hold her, which deeply bothered me because her weight had to reach four pounds before she could even leave the hospital. Victor played the grieving father with the emotionally disturbed wife role to the hilt to get as much attention as he could. Victor was such a sympathy junkie.

One day, on the good graces of a friend from Kingdom Hall, I was able to go to the hospital to see Yolanda while she watched Victoria. I tried as hard as I could to maintain a positive attitude about Yolanda's progress as it had been several months since the twins were born and I knew I couldn't survive losing Yolanda. When I walked into the unit, one of the nurses approached me with good news — I would finally be able to hold Yolanda! Her lungs became strong enough that she was able to breathe on her own without the help of chest tubes and was put on oxygen during the night. Tears welled up in my eyes as the nurse handed her to me. I thought about Little Susan and how I could be holding both of my babies now instead of one, but I put the thought out of my head so I could focus on Yolanda. I held her until her nostrils flared which meant she was struggling to breathe, so the nurse took her from me and put her back in the incubator and back on the oxygen. The doctor told me that if she got a little stronger, she would be able to go home in a couple of weeks. At least I had something positive to look forward to and I could put my plan into action to finally leave Victor.

Yolanda reached four pounds and started to get better. The hospital gave me the opportunity to spend the night with Yolanda while they trained me on infant CPR to make sure I would be comfortable taking care of her. On the night I was scheduled to stay in the hospital, I had no other choice but to leave Victoria with Victor and prayed to God to keep my baby safe until I got back. I packed a few things and Victor dropped me off at the hospital. Having the opportunity to spend the night in the hospital with Yolanda not only gave me a chance to bond with her, but it would be one night of peace and quiet without Victor. In addition to the infant CPR training, the doctors also trained me on how to operate the heart monitor and the oxygen tank because that was what Yolanda would be discharged with.

When morning came, it was time for Yolanda to be discharged from the hospital. I took care of the paperwork and was finally able to walk out of the hospital with my baby, but not without having to carry an oxygen tank on one shoulder and a heart monitor on the other. The doctors warned me of what I would have to go through at home with Yolanda; special formula, medications and how to operate the heart monitor in case she had apnea or bradycardia. With premature babies, apnea is a period that the baby stops breathing and bradycardia is when the baby's blood oxygen level drops.

During the time Yolanda was in the hospital, Victor didn't miss a beat with his selfish, self-centered, abusive ways. He still went to the clubs on Friday and sometimes Saturday night. That was good for me because I had no time to be concerned with Victor because I had more important things on my mind.

My first priority after bringing Yolanda home was to get her and Victoria on the same schedule. The hospital ran its tests on Yolanda at night, so she slept most of the day. In addition, it took me several sleepless weeks to get Yolanda's feeding and sleeping schedule to match Victoria's. Feeding them at the same time was challenging, as I would feed Victoria with one hand while she sat in her high chair and would hold and feed Yolanda with the other arm. Victoria loved playing the big sister and would say to me "My baby," pointing at Yolanda.

I knew for the sake of my children, I had to get out of North Carolina and back to New York before Victor killed me. But first, I had to take Yolanda to the doctor for her checkup and see if she was cleared to travel, then I would make sure to continue her care back in New York.

It was a Friday night and as usual, it was Victor's night to go to the club, so I put Victoria and Yolanda in the bed with me. I laid on the bed with the girls, I watched TV until I fell asleep because the only time I could sleep was when he wasn't there and the girls were asleep. At around two-thirty in the morning, the squeaky brakes of the car woke me up, which meant that Victor was home. I heard Victor come in the house, close the door and then a sound as if he dropped something on the floor. As I heard him walking up the stairs, I held my breath and prayed he didn't come into the bedroom. I sighed in relief when he went into the bathroom instead. The fear and panic of him coming into the bedroom caused my heart to beat rapidly and I started to sweat. Would he rape me again this time, while my children watched? That thought crossed my mind just before I heard him come out of the bathroom and walk back down the stairs. "Whew! I hope he just goes downstairs and stays there!" I thought to myself. Then I heard a huge noise that sounded like a person falling on the floor. Then I heard nothing. I strained my ear to hear if anything else was going on before I came out of the bedroom. Maybe this was a setup, I thought to myself. Maybe Victor was playing his games again. Fearing the worst, I took my chances. I opened the door to the bedroom and walked into the hallway.

"Victor?" I yelled. Nothing.

"Victor?" I yelled again. Nothing.

I slowly walked down the stairs and towards the kitchen. The back door was open and Victor lay on the floor with a huge bump on his head and a hammer lying next to him. I picked up the phone and called the MPs.

When the MP's came, I told them exactly what happened and what I saw. Then they took Victor outside and spoke to him while they waited for the ambulance to come. Although I wondered what was so private that they had to go outside to talk about it, I figured it was best that I stayed inside. I heard the ambulance pull up in front of the house and saw Victor get in. No one said anything to me — he just left. All the better. I didn't want to be involved in this game of Victor's, so I went back upstairs and got back into the bed with my daughters. I really didn't care what happened to him.

I was in the kitchen when I heard Victor come into the house a few hours later. He didn't have any shoes on, which I thought was strange.

"The MPs were nice enough to drop me off," he said.

I didn't even look at him because I really didn't care what happened to him. Then he continued talking.

"The doctor told me that whoever broke into the house and hit me with the hammer meant to kill me." Once again, he's telling me this as if I really cared. I would NEVER be that lucky, I thought. I had learned not to believe anything Victor said because he liked to stretch the truth. So, when he started talking, I had to dissect everything he said.

As he talked, several thoughts ran through my mind. First, it was strange that Victor didn't have any shoes on. Two, no one ever "broke into" the house while the girls and I were there alone. Three, if someone "meant" to kill Victor, they would have made sure he was dead before leaving the house. Four, if someone WAS in the house waiting for Victor, he/she/they were there with me and the girls! I shook my head and thought that Victor was saying all of this to scare me. This was impossible! I thought of all the stunts Victor pulled, all the games he played and concluded that no one was trying to "kill" him. Then he interrupted my thoughts.

"The MPs want us to come down to the station so they can ask us some more questions." This time, I answered.

"What for? Didn't they ask enough questions when they were here? I have two babies to take care of. I don't have time for this!"

"It won't take long," Victor said.

I stomped upstairs and got the girls ready so we could get this over with. Ever since Little Susan's death, Victor was dead to me. I kept my conversations with him to a minimum and I rarely acknowledged his presence. As far as Victor was concerned, I guess some attention is better than no attention.

We finally arrived at the Central Intelligence Division office of the military, which was their version of the Federal Bureau of Investigation. The agent walked up to me and introduced himself as Agent Dawson.*

"Would you mind stepping in this room so we can talk? I'll talk to your husband right after we're done." he told me.

I handed Yolanda to Victor then he took Victoria's hand and sat down in the waiting area.

"Don't worry, I'm not leaving you. I'll be right out here with the girls when you're done." Something didn't feel right to me about this whole situation.

When I sat down with Agent Dawson, I went into shock when he told me the reason I was there was because I tried to kill my husband! I spent the next three to four hours being interrogated by Agent Dawson as to why I would try to "kill" my husband. Agent Dawson even mentioned a young man I knew by the name of Richard,* who was the cousin of my half-sister and who joined the military but was at Fort Dix in Basic Training. The Agent created this elaborate scenario in his head that Richard and I were lovers and Richard travelled from Fort Dix, New Jersey to Fort Bragg, North Carolina in one night just to kill my husband! Victor knew about Richard from meeting him, but why drag him into this? Richard didn't have anything to do with this because we were just friends! This was becoming comical. Only thing was, I wasn't laughing.

I was tired, hungry and had to go to the bathroom. When I told Agent Dawson so, he told me I couldn't go anywhere. Although I had never been in trouble before, let alone inside a place like that, I knew about tactics like depriving someone of food, water and the bathroom in the hopes they would "crack" from watching crime shows like Hawaii Five-O. My head felt like it was going to split open from the horrible headache I had from not eating and at the same time feeling as if I was going to pee on myself because the pressure of my bladder against my C-section stitches was excruciating. Although this was my first encounter EVER with law enforcement and I was obviously scared, at the same time, I wanted to laugh too. Victor was trying to set me up in this elaborate war game of his! He had threatened to take the girls from me before, but this was ridiculous! Was he trying to get me arrested so he could take my daughters from me? I got angry as Agent Dawson walked out of the room over to the waiting area where Victor was, said a few words to him, then Victor walked out of the office with Victoria and Yolanda! That fucking bastard was leaving me there! Agent Dawson never intended to question Victor!

By the time Agent Dawson came back into the room, I no longer cared what he said or did as he made various attempts to catch me in a lie by asking all kinds of questions in different ways. How was I going to deal with this? While Agent Dawson wrote some things in his report, my mind went back to the time when Victor and I dated. He said things to me to impress me, such as his mother was such an important secretary in a law firm that she was driven home from work every night in a limousine. In addition, how he made it seem as if they were well to do because he lived on the Upper West Side. I also knew Victor liked to exaggerate.

I continued to dig into my memory about other things Victor told me about his experience in Basic Training too, including some of the tricks that the military used when the enemy was captured. Right then and there, I realized that in order for me to deal with this situation and not lose my head, I had to picture myself as the enemy that had been captured and Agent Dawson was trying to get me to confess with his barrage of questions.

The agent interrupted my train of thought again.

"Your husband tells me that you had an affair with Richard and that it was Richard who tried to kill him."

I may have been young, but I wasn't stupid and I needed to let the agent know this.

"Agent Dawson, first of all, there WAS no affair. Second, there is NO WAY Richard could leave Basic Training, where everyone knows when you eat, shit and sleep, drive seven hours to Ft. Bragg, TRY to kill my husband and drive seven hours back to Fort Dix without anyone knowing it!" I yelled back.

Now I was REALLY getting angry and could feel tears welling up in my eyes. I'm sure the agent thought my tears meant that I was about to confess, but I knew that if I let my anger and fear get the better of me, I would have confessed to something I didn't do just to get out of there. Then I continued yelling at him to the point other agents in the room turned around to look at us.

"Now's my turn to ask the questions! Where were YOU when my husband assaulted me when I was pregnant? I called the MPs when he assaulted me and they just left me in that house with him! Where were YOU when my daughter died?" The agent got quiet.

I knew I threw him off guard by saying that to him and he looked as if he tried to get his bearings.

"We're not here to talk about that," was all Agent Dawson could say.

Once I got a handle on the situation, it didn't take me long to realize this was one big mind game.

"Yes, let's talk about this Agent Dawson, because I'm sure your next set of questions would include why would I try to kill my husband. Well let me clear one thing up with you, Agent Dawson! With all the abuse I endured at the hands of my husband, including being CHOKED and STRANGLED while pregnant, being SHOT with a high-powered air gun while I was pregnant, SLAPPED, verbally abused and him causing the death of my daughter with no one to protect me, believe me, I would have done WAY MORE than just tap his stupid ass on the head with a hammer!"

Agent Dawson just stared at me. I noticed he was becoming increasingly agitated because he wasn't getting the answers from me that he was looking for. After several hours of playing his mind games, the agent realized that I had nothing to do with Victor being hit in the head with the hammer after all. Looking back on that experience, I didn't know that I had the right to walk out of there at anytime because they never charged me with anything. I sat there for hours for nothing. I finally came to the conclusion that Victor hit himself in the head with the hammer. It takes a sick person to do that to himself, just to set someone up for something they didn't do.

Agent Dawson became disgusted and told me I could leave. As I was walked out, I spoke to Agent Dawson one last time with an indignant tone.

"So tell me Agent Dawson, what makes you think my husband didn't hit himself in the head to frame me?"

"Because he's an upstanding service member, that's why," Agent Dawson replied.

That was all I needed to hear. As I walked outside the office, I saw Victor in the car with Yolanda and Victoria. I got in and slammed the door.

"Why did you leave me?" I tried not to yell because I didn't want to upset the girls.

"Because the agent told me I could leave — that you were going to be there for a while and I could pick you up in a few hours," Victor said.

I shut my mouth as we pulled off in the car. I knew EXACTLY what was going on — I was becoming a puppet in Victor's performance called our life and he was pulling the strings. Just a little while longer of this bullshit I thought to myself as the car pulled off ....

Chapter 17

Summer 1988 — Your Place Is
With Your Husband

Victor wanted to take a trip New York to visit his mother so she could see the girls. Translation — Victor was going to New York to see his mother and I was going along to take care of the babies. It hardly bothered me that Susan was so shallow that she couldn't come to North Carolina to see Yolanda in the hospital or to Little Susan's funeral. She never called me to see how I was feeling and I suspect it was out of guilt because she knew from day one that Victor was hurting me.

On the days leading up to our trip to New York, Yolanda was cleared for travel by her doctor and I figured this would be the perfect opportunity for me to leave Victor. When it came time for us to leave, I just simply wouldn't go back with him. I knew he would have no other choice but to go back to North Carolina because if he didn't, he would be considered AWOL — Absent Without Leave. On the day we were to leave, we packed up the kids into the car along with our luggage and got on the road for the long drive to New York. The drive was pretty solemn and quiet. Victor was volatile and unpredictable, so I didn't want to get into any arguments with him on the road for fear that he may crash the car with all of us in it. I prayed that we would have a safe trip without incident and I did my best to focus all of my attention on making sure Victoria and Yolanda were comfortable during the ride.

We made arrangements with my mother to stay at her house, so when we arrived in New York eight hours later, we went straight there.

As soon as we got inside and said "Hi" to my Mom, Victor told me he was taking the girls over to his mother's house because she had cooked dinner in anticipation of his visit. When I told my Mom that we were going to Susan's house and would be back, Victor pulled me over to the side and whispered in my ear.

"Where do you think you're going?" I looked at him, clearly angry and very agitated.

"You said we were going to your mother's house for dinner."

Victor replied with a slight smirk.

"I said that my mother cooked dinner for ME and the girls. You weren't invited." The fucking nerve of this man!

"How are you going to tell me that you're taking MY kids to YOUR mother's house and I'm not invited?" I said to him.

"My mother didn't invite you. Why can't I just spend time with my mother without you around? I'll be back soon."

There was nothing more I could say. He picked up Yolanda, her heart monitor and oxygen tank, grabbed Victoria's hand, closed the door and left. I couldn't stop him from taking the girls although I worried about Yolanda. Victor didn't know anything about taking care of Yolanda, didn't know anything about her medications or what to do if the heart monitor went off. I tried to occupy myself with the thought that in a few days he would be going back to North Carolina without us and I could finally be free of him. When my mother asked why I didn't go with Victor and the girls, I simply told her that I didn't feel like going and that I was tired. When he and the girls left, I went into my old room to lie down and think. I thought about my decision to leave Victor and whether it was the right one. Once I made the decision to stay in New York, I didn't want to go back because if I did, I knew the abuse would get worse. I thought about everything I went through with Victor and had to be brutally honest with myself because the decisions I made right then and there would have an impact on me and my girls for the rest of our lives. All kinds of questions ran around in my head like a hamster in a wheel so I could make a decision to stay with Victor or to stay in New York and rebuild my life.

If I decided to stay with Victor, what would life be like for me and the girls once we got back to North Carolina? Could I leave Victor, continue to live in North Carolina and be safe? Since he has already put my life in jeopardy once already, would he finally succeed in killing me? What would happen to my girls if something happened to me? Did Victor love me? Should a man treat a woman like that if he says he loves her? Was Victor going to change? Was I going against my religious upbringing by leaving him and getting a divorce? Should I give him a chance? Did I want to live the rest of my life with him abusing me? Did I want my daughters to learn that it was okay for a woman to be mistreated by watching him abuse me? Would he start abusing the girls? Would he start abusing Yolanda because it was a constant reminder to him of Little Susan? Could I honestly look Victor in the face every day and continue to try to have a life with him although he was responsible for the death of one of my children? Will we ever know what it would be like to be happy? What kind of psychological or emotional problems would my daughters have if I stayed? What would I do or say to my daughters if they were in a similar situation? If I decided to stay in New York, what kind of job could I get with only a high school education? Would the girls and I be safe in New York or safer living in another state? Should we stay in a shelter instead of with my mother? How do I go about getting a divorce? Would Victor come back to New York just to harass me because he was mad that I left?

I knew I no longer loved Victor. When I weighed the pros and cons of my situation, I realized that he wasn't going to change, that he didn't love me or the girls, he would eventually kill me and we would never be happy. I came to the conclusion that I was going to stick to my guns and stay in New York. I didn't like the prospect of my daughters and me living with my mother, but I figured it would only be temporary until I found a job and got on my feet. If we were going to have a shot at being happy, we needed to be away from Victor. As I continued to lie on my bed, I sighed in relief that I had finally made my decision, although I knew I had a long way to go.

I was so wrapped up in my own thoughts that I didn't remember how much time went by before I heard the doorbell and Victor was back with the girls. They were happy to see me as he handed Yolanda to me and Victoria hugged my leg. They were obviously tired, so I gave them a bath and put them to bed in one of my mother's extra bedrooms. I wanted to sleep in the room with the girls but Victor wouldn't hear of it. He wanted me to sleep in the bed with him and I really didn't want to do that because I knew that he wanted sex. He had already raped me once and I clearly wasn't interested in him touching me so I had to figure out a way to get out of having sex with him. Therefore, I stayed awake in the living room and talked to my mother in the hopes that he would get tired of waiting and go to sleep. The countdown began; one night down, two more to go.

The day came when "we" were supposed to leave to go back to North Carolina, as Victor had to report for duty the next day. I threw clothes into the suitcase to make him believe that I was packing. Some time went by before I went in the living room and sat down on the couch and watched TV while my mother was in the kitchen cooking food for us to take on the road.

"Come on, we've got to leave!" Victor yelled.

I mustered the courage to squeeze the words out of my mouth.

"I'm not going back with you Victor."

"What the fuck! Come on Ivette, stop playing these fucking games. Let's go!" he yelled even louder.

When he realized I wasn't getting off the couch, he turned and walked towards the kitchen where my mother was.

"Ivette is telling me she's not going back with me," I heard him say to my mother.

Such a whining bitch! Here we go again, I thought. He was going to use the old "you don't wanna play with me so I'm gonna tell on you and make you play with me" trick so my mother would make me leave with him. I was already prepared for Victor manipulating my mother so, in turn, he could manipulate me. My mother walked out of the kitchen and sat down on the couch across from me in the living room. Victor took his place next to my mother. While Victor leaned back into the couch, my mother leaned forward. The stage was set and I was prepared to stand up for myself.

"What's this I hear you're not going back with Victor?" my mother asked.

"Ma, I'm not going back down there with him. If you make me leave with him, he'll kill me." Victor put his hand over his mouth as if to stifle a giggle.

"You're married and Victor is your husband. Your place is with him. Besides, he is those girls' father and they need their father growing up!" my mother said with an authoritative tone.

I could feel the tears coming and although my resolve was starting to weaken, I was determined to stay strong. What was her problem that she believed Victor over me? Why was she bullying me and talking to me as if I was a child?

As a child, I never disrespected my mother by being defiant nor raising my voice to her. I always did what I was told, but I was no longer a child because I was a grown woman, with two children, married to an abusive man and I needed help. If there was any time for me to be defiant, it was now. I no longer cared if I was being disrespectful. For God's sake, this was my life I was talking about!

"Why should I stay? So he can teach the girls to let a man hit on them and degrade them? Ma, he abuses me, he hits me. He made me lose my baby, your granddaughter. Why should I have to go back with him? How much can he care about his children if he makes them watch me be abused?"

I couldn't bring myself to tell my mother about the time when Victor grabbed his crotch and made that comment about shutting Victoria up. I got even more frustrated because Victor sat with his hand over his mouth and giggled, and it annoyed me that my mother couldn't see him.

"Because he's your husband," my mother replied.

Then Victor chimed in, "Ma'am, I know I did some horrible things to Ivette. I know I was wrong and I told Ivette this, but she won't listen to me. She is the mother of my children and I promise I will never hit her again." Man, have I heard that before!

I finally thought that my mother was going to stand up for me, that she would see the seriousness of the situation, but I was quickly disappointed. My mother ended up defending Victor.

"Ivette, if Victor says he's not going to hit you again, why don't you just give him a chance?" I couldn't believe what I was hearing.

"Because he made me lose my baby!" I screamed. Victor tightened his hand over his mouth as if he couldn't contain himself.

It seemed as if my mother forgot what I just said to her and I had to remind her again.

"Ma, if you make me go back to North Carolina with that man, you will have to bury me!" My mother just shook her head.

"Don't be ridiculous. You're going to go back to North Carolina with your husband because your place is with him and you can't stay here!"

After everything that has happened and with what I just told her, I felt betrayed that she would take Victor's side against me. I quickly realized I had no allies, no one on my side, no home. My mother wore me down with her bullying, despite me standing my ground with her. Still crying and feeling defeated, I got off the couch, went into the bedroom and packed my suitcase. Victor stayed in the living room and talked with my mother for a little while longer before he walked into the bedroom. God knows what else he told her.

"I told you you could never leave me. What on this earth made you think you could?" Victor whispered in my ear. I just looked at him and rolled my eyes at him; he may have won a few battles, but that did not mean he won the war! I had to go back to the drawing board and figure out another plan. If at first you don't succeed....

The ride back to North Carolina was even more solemn than before. I didn't know what to do. I had no job, no money and my own mother wouldn't believe me. I was trying to leave my abuser! What my mother didn't know was that by making me go back to Victor, she jeopardized my safety. My only option was to stay at her house and I had no Plan B in case that didn't work. I needed time to regroup and gather my thoughts so I could figure out what I was going to do next.

A few days after we got back to North Carolina, Victor began acting nice towards me. He talked to me about trading in the two cars he had to get a new one, as if I really cared what he did with those cars.

"I want to make a fresh start and try to make things up to you for everything I've done to you. I want to get you a new car with no strings attached." I knew that there was no such thing with Victor as "no strings attached."

I briefly thought that maybe he was trying to change, but at the same time, something still gnawed at me that something wasn't right and I shouldn't trust him. Days later, we went to the dealership to let me pick out a new car — a four-door black Hyundai SE. We went inside to fill out the paperwork and he signed where it said "Owner" and I signed where it said "Co-Signer." I didn't think much of it at the time, but I later found out the hard way that "Co-Signer" is not the same as "Co-Owner." Once again, I should have listened to my instincts about Victor.

Approximately two weeks after we got the car, I told Victor I wanted to go and visit Tracey so she could see the girls without him. I guess he figured I would drive off and leave him again, so he "kindly" offered to drive me. I knew that he really wanted to brag to Harry about the car he just "bought" me. I guess he wanted to prove to Harry that he was trying to change by treating me better too. We loaded the girls into the car and headed toward Tracey and Harry's house. When we got there, Victor stayed outside in the car with the girls while I went inside, which was an indication that we weren't going to be there long. He knew that Tracey didn't like him, especially after what happened with Little Susan and Yolanda. I was inside for a few minutes before Tracey and I came back outside and stood in front of her house to continue our conversation. Victor interrupted our conversation.

"Come on Ivette, let's go!"

I looked at Tracey, sighed and rolled my eyes. So much for him changing. I had really had enough of Victor's shit.

"I'm not ready yet Victor," I replied.

Still, he did not get out of the car and decided to yell again out the window.

"I said, come the fuck on and let's go!"

I was getting annoyed and embarrassed at the same time.

"I said I'm not ready yet!" I yelled back.

Victor got out of the car, walked over to where I stood, grabbed me by the arm and pulled me towards the car. We struggled for a bit and

Tracey yelled at him to let me go. Victoria saw all of this from her car seat and started to cry. Although Yolanda was in an infant seat and I couldn't see her, she started crying because Victoria was crying. Tracey yelled at Victor again.

"Let her go Victor!"

While I'm screaming for Victor to let me go, he spun me around with my back towards him, put both arms undermine and locked his fingers around my head, then pushed me towards the car. He was huffing and puffing because I was still fighting him to let me go.

"I told you to let's fucking go! You don't fucking listen, fucking bitch!" he yelled in my ear.

I couldn't get out of his grip and had no way of making him let me go. Tracey was still yelling at him to turn me loose. I lifted my feet and used the heels of my shoes to scrape at his shins, hoping he would let me go. Just then, with Victor's left arm still under my left arm, he took his right arm, hooked it under my right leg, lifted me up in the air, turned me sideways and upside down, slamming me head-first onto the concrete. I just laid there stunned, dizzy, and unable to get up. I heard Tracey screaming as she ran past me to where Victor was standing.

"Why did you have to do that to her Victor? She didn't do nothin' to you!" Tracey came to where I was to try to help me up.

"C'mon Ivette, I'll take you inside the house, then I'm calling the police whether you like it or not!"

As she tried to get me off the ground and I tried to push myself up with my left arm, a bolt of pain shot through me. That's when I noticed my left shoulder was pushed in at an angle towards my face that didn't look natural. By then, I panicked and was crying hysterically.

"Tracey I can't get up. Look at my shoulder!"

Tracey took her time helping me.

"It's okay gurl, try to get up so I can get you in the house."

While Victor stood there huffing and puffing with his hands at his sides balled into fists, Tracey managed to help me up and inside the house. Once again, I found myself in yet another situation where the girls were crying and I couldn't get to them because I was hurt.

Tracey was beside herself with anger while she helped me sit on the couch.

"I don't care what you say, Ivette, I'm going to call the cops! He didn't have any right to do that to you."

As Tracey picked up the phone, I grabbed her arm and said through clenched teeth, "You can call the cops, but call my mother first please."

She agreed and I gave her my mother's number to call. Tracey identified herself and told my mother briefly, what happened. Then she gave the phone to me. This was another one of the few times in my life I ever raised my voice to my mother.

"I hope you're happy now! I told you that if you sent me back down here with Victor that he was going to kill me. I was trying to tell you that he was lying about not putting his hands on me anymore! But you wouldn't believe me! I told you that you would have to bury me! I hope you believe me now!" My mother was quiet the whole time.

"Oh my Lord!" was all she said before I hung up on her.

I gave the phone back to Tracey so she could call the ambulance next and she told them what happened. Minutes later, the ambulance arrived with the police right behind them. When Tracey helped me up to go outside to the ambulance, the ambulance worker met us at the door and helped me back towards the couch to examine me. He proceeded to tell me that he was taking me to the hospital to get my shoulder checked out. As he and Tracey helped me up and out the door towards the ambulance, I assessed what was going on outside.

Victor was leaning against the car with his arms crossed as if he didn't do anything as usual and the cops were talking to him. Because Victor never accepted responsibility for his actions, I'm sure he was somehow blaming me for this. He didn't seem concerned with the fact that the girls were still in the car crying and Yolanda's heart monitor was going off. Other times when Victor abused me, it was in private where there were no consequences. But this time, there was no way he could talk his way out of this because Tracey saw everything. Tracey stormed to where Victor and the cops were and pointed her finger at Victor.

"I saw everything! I saw this bastard pick her up and slam her down on the ground!" she said.

As I sat in the back of the ambulance, an officer came over and

took my statement then took a statement from Tracey. Since this incident happened off base, he asked me if I wanted to go to Cape Fear
Valley Medical Center or go on base to Womack. I decided that I would
go to Womack because if I went Cape Fear, they would bill me for the
hospital visit. Afterwards, Tracey jumped into the ambulance with me
for yet another trip to Womack Army Medical Center.

When the ambulance arrived at the hospital, I was taken out and
wheeled into the emergency room. By then, my arm felt was red and
swollen and my shoulder was still pushed in at an awkward angle towards my face. As Tracey and I waited in the emergency room, the doctor came in and spoke to me. I told him what happened and Tracey
confirmed everything. The doctor looked at my arm and tried to move
it. A jolt of pain shot through my body.

"We'll have to X-ray your shoulder to see what damage was done,"
the doctor said.

I had no idea where Victor or my daughters were as I was wheeled
into the X-ray room. After taking a few X-rays, the doctor explained to
me that there are three ligaments in everyone's shoulder — one in the
front, one at the top of your shoulder that holds down your collarbone
and one in the back, across your shoulder blade. He continued to explain to me that when Victor slammed me on the ground, he separated
my shoulder, ripped all three ligaments, which caused them to snap like
rubber bands, including the one that held my collarbone down. The
doctor sighed before he continued.

"You're going to have to have surgery to fix your ligaments and we
have to wait a year for the ligaments to heal before we repair it. The surgery would leave a foot long scar down your back and there's no guarantee that you'll have full use of your arm after the surgery."

I sat there processing what the doctor just told me. Where were the
girls and I going to stay for a whole year? I couldn't go back to living
with Victor for another minute, let alone another year!

"Doctor, if I stay in North Carolina, I won't live long enough to
have the surgery!" I said to him.

He just looked at me with a dazed look, as if he didn't completely
comprehend what I just said. He didn't bother to offer me any other

options as far as a safe place to stay.

Tracey, visibly upset from seeing what Victor did to me, shook her head as she listened to the doctor. I knew Victor didn't like Tracey and he would somehow blame Tracey for all of this, as he liked to blame others for his actions. I tried to focus my attention back to the situation at hand and asked the doctor if I needed a cast on my arm. He decided that a sling was better to immobilize it.

"Is there a friend you can stay with to help you?" The doctor asked.

"She can stay with me," Tracey chimed in.

I didn't want to be a burden on Tracey and Harry with me and not one but two babies in their home. But, I did need somewhere safe to go to have time to figure things out. After getting a prescription for a pain killer, Tracey and I walked out of the emergency room towards the waiting room where Victor, Victoria and Yolanda were. Tracey lightly touched me on the shoulder.

"I'm going to take you to your house so you can get some clothes for you and the girls," she said, all the while glaring at Victor. I said nothing as I took Victoria from him, Tracey took Yolanda, and we walked out. He didn't say a word.

I knew I needed help with the girls and was glad Tracey was there with me. I was able to pick Victoria up with one arm and swing her on my hip to carry her around and when I did that, she would say "Wheeee" like it was a roller-coaster ride. Yolanda was different, because she was still tiny and fragile and I couldn't pick her up with one hand like Victoria, so Tracey helped me more so with Yolanda. As I lay down in the bed with the girls, I tried to figure out what I was going to do. I couldn't stay at Tracey and Harry's house forever. I couldn't stay in North Carolina because I wasn't safe there either. While I lay in the bed, Tracey knocked on the door. When she came in, she had the phone in her hand.

"It's your mother."

I wondered how my mother got Tracey's phone number and figured once again that Victor had talked to my mother to "tell on me" again and gave her Tracey's number. I took the phone from her.

"Hello Ma," I said, my voice dull and flat.

"What are you doing at Tracey's house?" my mother said.

From the tone of her voice, I could tell she was angry. I wondered what Victor said to her.

"Ma, my shoulder is messed up and I need help with the girls," I told her.

My mother started again, only this time she was yelling.

"Victor told me all about your friend Tracey and how she's putting ideas in your head. He also told me that he's trying really hard to make this work and Tracey keeps putting her two cents in and you keep listening to her." So, that's what he told her! What does any of that have to do with my shoulder being broken?

"Ma, if you can explain to me how Victor breaking my shoulder is his way of trying to make this work, I would appreciate it. Tracey is not putting ideas in my head. I can see clearly what's going on and I'm not stupid. Tracey is helping me with the kids and I appreciate all the help she's giving me because I can't even change a diaper without help," I replied.

She cut me off as if she didn't hear a word I just said. My mother's lack of support and not wanting to get involved amazed me.

"You don't let NOBODY get between you and your husband! And you NEVER leave your home! Now, you pack your things and go home to your husband!" she screamed.

As usual, my mother was trying to bully me again and I was getting tired of it.

"Well maybe if somebody got between me and my husband, Little Susan would still be alive and I wouldn't be hurt now," I said before slamming the phone down.

I felt as if someone stabbed me in the back with a hot knife and gave it a good twist. After hanging up, I told Tracey about my conversation with my mother.

"Gurl, what's wrong with yo' Mama? Can't she see that Victor is pulling the wool over her eyes? Harry could never pull a stunt like that with MY family!"

I just sighed. "Tracey, I don't know what's wrong with everybody these days. Why doesn't anyone believe me? I knew Victor would eventually call my mother. And I have to tell you, you and Harry have been a Godsend to me and the girls. You were the only one that did believe me and Victor couldn't scare away. And, I thank God that I have you as a friend."

I felt the need to tell her how important she was to me just in helping me get through this tough time in my life. I got angry at myself for letting my mother bully me into going back to Victor and I hated it when she yelled at me because it made me feel like a little kid, incapable of making decisions for myself. But I also knew that no one was looking out for my safety but me. Tracey broke my train of thought.

"Gurl, I would do anything for you. Victor is an asshole and I don't like him. You can't stay at that house with him anymore. That man is going to kill you. You have to do something!" she said.

"Yeah, I know," I said, as I lay back down on the bed. Tracey could see that I was confused about this, so she closed the door to the room to give me some privacy.

When I got back to the house a couple of days later, Victor announced that he wasn't going to bother me. He even slept on the couch while I slept in the bedroom upstairs with the girls. My shoulder still hurt like hell and I tried to take care of the girls as best I could despite the pain and discomfort. I made it my business to make sure the girls were fed, bathed and asleep before I barricaded us in the room for the night to avoid any further confrontations with Victor. The panic attacks came more frequently when I heard the squeaky brakes of the new car, which meant Victor was home. Each day I prayed that that wasn't the day he would come home and start with me, or that he would take advantage of the fact that my arm was in a sling and he would try to hurt me again.

One thing I realized about Victor was that he would always attack me when I was in a position where I couldn't defend myself; while I was pregnant, after I had the twins, when he raped me and now that my arm was in a sling. On those nights I spent in the bedroom alone with the girls, I stayed awake most of the time on alert just in case Victor decided to break into the bedroom in the middle of the night and either assault me or rape me again. Most of the time, my mind went back to the night

I gave birth to Yolanda and Little Susan, of all those times he abused me physically and emotionally and of Little Susan's death.

As I lay in the bed, I took my time to carefully analyze all the things Victor said and did to me and realized I couldn't see the forest for the trees. Emotionally and psychologically, Victor kept me in a constant state of confusion so I couldn't think clearly. He knew everything about me and used it to his advantage, yet kept things about himself hidden. Victor had the "if it's a choice between me and you, it's gonna be me" attitude. I needed to examine my situation from the perspective of the person on the outside looking in. Although this was difficult to do, it wasn't impossible.

I learned several things about Victor:

First, I knew he liked to exaggerate or make up stories to put himself in a favorable light, even if that meant lying on someone else. For example, when he told me his family was well-to-do.

Second, he believed he was entitled to do whatever he wanted to me. For example, raping me because he could get away with it.

Third, I have witnessed Victor exploiting others to gain an advantage or gain sympathy. For example, when he told people at his job that Little Susan died in his arms when she didn't.

Fourth, the only emotion I've ever seen Victor exhibit was anger. For example, when Victor's record player stopped working, he got frustrated trying to fix it, so he smashed it on the floor.

Fifth, Victor made it clear to me that he was selfish and only his needs mattered. He never put the needs of his family above his own. For example, he bought one car to drive to work, one car to drive to the club and I couldn't drive either of them.

Sixth, he has painted a bad picture of me to others just to gain sympathy. For example, when he told people at my daughter's funeral that I was "losing my mind."

Seventh, Victor was unable to accept the feelings, needs, preferences, priorities and choices of others. For example, when I told him I wanted to take birth control and he told me he didn't want me "putting that shit in my body."

And the list goes on. I didn't know it at the time, but there was a name for someone like Victor — Narcissist.

As I drifted off to sleep with my arms around my girls, I put these mental notes in the back of my mind for future reference to help me figure out a way to leave Victor.

Chapter 18

Fall 1988 — Gotta Go

My mother called me sometime later in the month to remind me that my sister Bernice's wedding was in a couple of weeks and to ask if we were coming. I hadn't planned on being back in North Carolina by then, so I told her we would come to New York on the weekend of the wedding. That would be the perfect time for me to leave Victor! Only this time, I wouldn't let my mother bully me into going back. It didn't concern me at the time that my mother's attention was more focused on my younger sister than on what I was going through in North Carolina which meant that she was distracted and that was a good thing. I had a hard time accepting my mother's perception of what marriage was supposed to be like; that we as women do whatever is necessary to keep the family together and bear the cross of her family's sins. I believed had to live with the abuse because I was Victor's wife and I had no other choice. As far as where I would live, I had a choice of either living with my mother or staying in a shelter with my kids. Neither was easy choice to make, so I decided that living with my mother would be better than living in a shelter.

When we prepared for our second trip to New York, Victor didn't notice I packed more clothes than what was needed and I secretly hoped he wouldn't catch on. I figured I could eventually go back to North Carolina later to get the rest of me and the girls' things, although I really didn't care about any of my stuff. I just wanted to make sure I had everything I needed for the girls and I would make do with what I had.

We finally arrived in New York and, as usual, we stayed with my mother. Same as last time, Victor went to his mother's house for dinner, took the girls, and didn't invite me. I wasn't surprised. Susan may have believed that speaking to me would force her to admit all the things her son had done to me and I'm sure she wasn't ready for that. My sister and her fiancé had planned a big wedding with about five hundred guests, which was a grand wedding compared to Victor and me getting married at City Hall. I had naturally assumed that I was going to be my sister's matron-of-honor but was curious as to why she never called me to talk about it. I figured I would be prepared anyway, so I bought an inexpensive royal blue gown to match her wedding color. Then came the surprise, when just a few days before the wedding, she called me.

"You can't be in my wedding. The elders told me you couldn't be in the wedding because you married someone outside of your faith and you weren't in good standing in the congregation. My future sister-in-law will be my matron-of-honor."

I was very disappointed, but I didn't argue with her. I was still going to my sister's wedding and I was still going to wear the blue gown I bought.

On the day of my sister's wedding, Victor drove and got lost on the way, so we only made it to the reception. To this day, I think he did that on purpose.

While we were there, I tried to keep my distance from him although he tried to portray us as the happy couple to everyone else. Since he picked up on my mood, he interacted with Victoria by getting her to dance with him on the floor, while Yolanda was happily passed around from one member of my family to another because it was the first time anyone ever saw her. After a while, I stopped trying to keep up with which family member had her and tried to enjoy myself. I eventually found Yolanda in the arms of my younger cousin. He was so fond of her that he didn't want to give her back to me, so I let him hold her a little while longer.

During the reception dinner, I became more and more preoccupied with what I was going to do when it came time for Victor to leave and go back to North Carolina than I was with my sister and her lavish wedding. We were only going to be in New York for three days and were leaving the day after my sister's wedding. I tried not to feel bad as these Jehovah's Witnesses were looking down on me in judgment and didn't speak to me because of my "standing" in the Kingdom Hall for marrying Victor. Not only did a lot of them watch my sister and me grow up, but we grew up with their kids as well. As disappointing as that was, I had more important things to worry about. The next day was the day Victor was leaving without me and the girls. After getting back to my mother's house from the wedding, Victor packed his bags and put them by the front door so we could just get up and leave the next morning. I decided to play my hand out until then.

I walked around my mother's house with the biggest secret in the world and no one knew but me — that I was going to finally break away from Victor once and for all. For a change, I was actually in a good mood. I felt as if my life was going to take a turn for the better because if I stayed with Victor, I would be nothing more than an abused wife with no hopes, prospects, or choices for the future. That night I tried to sleep, but couldn't because I wondered what would happen the next morning when I told Victor and my mother that I wasn't going back to North Carolina. I was prepared to fight because my life and my soul, as well as the lives and souls of my girls, depended on it.

Morning finally came and Victor got dressed so "we" could get on the road. I diddled around the house until the last possible minute until I was ready to tell him I wasn't going back with him.

"Ivette, what's taking you so long to get your shit together?" he yelled at me.

"I have to finish getting the girls' things together!" I said to him.

Then I waited another half hour or so. When the time was right, I went in the bedroom where he was and dropped the bomb — again.

"Victor, I'm not going back with you. And if you think you can get my mother to make me, go ahead and try it; it won't work. I told you one day that if you didn't treat me better, that you were going home to an empty house. I'm NEVER going back to you, EVER!"

It felt good to finally say that to Victor, but he wasn't moved by my words and didn't take me seriously.

"I don't have time for your fuckin' games Ivette!, now come on and let's go!" he said.

This time, I wasn't backing down, even if he got everyone in the building on his side. I stood in front of him and looked him squarely in the face.

"Just get in your car and go back down South with your diseased hoes! I'm not goin' no fuckin where!" I told him.

Being the little bitch that he was, he ran down the hallway to where my mother was. I heard him tell my mother I was "playing games" again. I silently chuckled to myself. I didn't care anymore. Next, I heard what sounded like two sets of footsteps coming down the hallway — I knew it was Victor and my mother and when she got to the bedroom where I was, she had that disgusted look on her face I knew so well. As my mother stood in front of me, Victor promptly took his place behind her. I already knew what he was up to and I was prepared for it.

"Ivette, I told you before that your place was with your husband! Stop this nonsense and pack your things! You know Victor has got to be back at work in the morning!"

As usual, Victor put his hand over his mouth and started to giggle. I didn't pay him any mind as I looked my mother dead in her eyes. I wanted to let her know she couldn't intimidate me anymore.

"I don't care what you say or do Ma but I'm not going back with Victor. If you think he's such a great guy, you're free to marry him yourself!"

My mother was speechless as she stood there and looked at me. As she walked out of the room towards the back of the house, I knew she finally realized it was no use to make me go back with Victor. Even more so, Victor realized very quickly that this was a battle he had lost, so he huffed and sucked his teeth, picked up his bags, walked past me out the door and I happily closed the door behind him.

The next part of my battle was about to begin. Once Victor was gone, I had to listen to my mother yell at me about leaving him, and how my daughters needed a father, so on and so forth. She felt I should have stayed with Victor no matter what he did to me, just so my daugh-

ters could have a father. I was tired of her yelling and screaming at me
and defending Victor. I had two daughters to raise and that's what I intended to do. I also knew in advance that the next few days were going
to be the hardest and that Victor and my mother were going to put the
screws to me to make me give in as I had done in the past. But this
time, I was prepared for both of them. What neither Victor nor I realized was that while he was abusing me, he was actually making me
stronger.

Just like clockwork, Victor started calling my mother's house two to
three times a night. Since I didn't bother to pick up the phone, my
mother would tell Victor I was busy. When called back hours later, she
would tell him the same thing. Meanwhile, I was determined not to let
my mother's rantings get me down either, so I learned to tune her out.
Because I didn't want me or the girls to be a burden on her, I let her
know that I would start looking for a job. About a week or so later, I
found a job with a temp agency making minimum wage. It wasn't
enough to pay for my own apartment, but I could at least take care of
me and the girls because Victor wasn't sending me any money for them.

I was glad to be back in New York and was feeling that I was finally
making some progress with my life and was getting Victor out of my
system. I knew I didn't love him anymore and knowing that made me
strong enough to continue standing my ground and not go back to him.
I came home from work one day and the phone rang. I picked it up, not
thinking that it could be Victor.

"Ivette, it's Victor."

"What do you want?" I spat back.

"You warned me that one day I would come home to an empty
house and I did. It's lonely here without you and the kids."

I knew this was another one of Victor's games. Only this time, I
wasn't playing with him.

"You mean you don't have anyone to abuse," I shot back. He acted
as if he didn't hear me. I could hear him sniffling, as if he were crying. I
reached for one of my mental notes about Victor being incapable of
feeling empathy and decided he was faking tears as a ploy to get to my
emotions.

"You and those girls are the best things that have ever happened to me and I didn't realize it until you were gone. You and the girls have been gone for a month and that's long enough because it's time for you to come back home now." I let him know his tears didn't move me.

"I can clearly see that you're not taking me seriously! So now we're the best things that have ever happened to you? Newsflash for you Victor! We're not "things," we're humans — humans that feel the physical injuries and humiliation you inflict on us. Humans that are affected by every nasty thing you do. Now that you have one less child, now we're the best "things" that has ever happened to you? You were so worried that all your money was going out the window with a wife and three kids. You think things are going to be better with a wife and two kids? I will never make my home with an asshole because my home is in New York!" Then I hung up on him.

As soon as I put the receiver back on the hook, it rang again. I answered, knowing it was him. Only this time, his tone wasn't somber like before. He was in a much different mood.

"You think you can leave me? You ain't got nothing. You won't have those girls long, I promise you! You will never be able to raise them better than I can! You're going to regret leaving me!"

After listening to Victor's threats and knowing he would make good on them, I knew I had to stay strong. I couldn't afford to let him intimidate me into going back to him. Now he sounded like a man desperate to hold onto possessions that were being taken away from him. In addition, he did whatever he had to do to instill fear, maintain power, and re -enforce control over me. I had no idea of what was about to come.

Chapter 19

Winter 1989 — Amusing Himself

W hen Victor realized that I wasn't coming back, he would come to New York to amuse himself at my expense. He told me once in a phone call that he would give me the car and make the payments until I could make them on my own, then transfer the registration over to me. The only thing that happened was that he brought the car to me in New York, then told me he didn't have any money. So, I ended up making the payments. I became frustrated when I asked him several times about holding up his end of the deal. Instead, he strung me along by telling me would take care of it, only for weeks to go by and not do anything. There were even times I went to use the car and it wasn't parked on the street where I left it. Then it would mysteriously re-appear hours later. That was because Victor came to New York and took the car without telling me. I finally confronted him about it.

"Victor, you told me you were going to transfer the car registration to me. I can't continue to drive a car with your name on the registration. What's going on?"

"What are you talking about? That car is mine! I'm just letting you use it!" he said back.

"But both of us own the car." I replied.

"No, I'm the owner and you are the co-signer! Yeah, I told you that I would make payments on the car, but that was only if you had stayed with me! Since you didn't stay with me, well then…."

Geez, was there any end to his madness? He knew I was making just enough money to take care of me and the girls and he knew the car payments were putting a financial strain on me.

"Fine, then if you won't transfer the registration, then I'll stop making car payments!" I spat back. Then the tone of his voice changed.

"Ivette, don't start fuckin' around! If you stop making payments, you'll mess up my credit!"

After all this and the only thing he worried about was his credit? I responded to the issue of his credit by hanging up on him. When I look back on that situation, that was an example of financial abuse. Victor had no need for a co-signer because his credit was intact. Instead, he used it as a way to manipulate me into staying with him.

Even though I now lived New York, I still kept in touch with Tracey. She was the only real friend I ever had and she understood why I had to leave North Carolina. About a month later, I decided to drive to North Carolina to get the rest of the girls' things from the house, especially the crib for Yolanda to sleep in. I didn't care about the furniture or even my things. I had heard stories of the women taking EVERYTHING out the house when they left, including all the money in the bank, but that wasn't my style because I wasn't going to take anything that didn't belong to me. I called Tracey to let her know what I was doing and if I could stay at her house and get some rest before I got back on the road. I knew I could trust that she wouldn't tell Victor what I was doing.

"Gurl, you sure can!" she said.

I took a Friday off from work and left early that morning. I knew Victor had physical training at a certain time and then he would come home, change, and be to work by 9 a.m. There was a chance that he would come back to the house for lunch at noon, so I only had a three-hour window to pack up the Hyundai with the girls' things and get to Tracey's house.

I left the girls with my mother so I could quickly go down there, get my things and get back. I left New York at about midnight and ended up on Ft. Bragg at 7 a.m., right on schedule. I ate breakfast and spent some time at Little Susan's grave so I would arrive at the house by nine-thirty, a half an hour after Victor left for work. As I sat at Little Susan's grave to say goodbye, the gaping hole left in my heart by her death seemed to be getting bigger and bigger by the second. I made certain promises to myself that day that I intended to keep; that I would NEVER let another man do to me what Victor had done to me; that I was going to enjoy my life and that I was going to raise Victoria and Yolanda violence-free.

Nine-thirty came and it was time for me to drive to the house. I slowly and carefully drove from the cemetery to Spear Drive to make sure I didn't run into Victor going to work. I parked the car near the house and walked up to the door. Thank goodness, Victor hadn't changed the locks, so I was able to get inside. I knew I was running against the clock so I went upstairs into what used to be the girls' bedroom. I passed by the main bedroom, only to see another woman's things there. Victor had moved another woman into the house! I just shook my head. I wasn't surprised. But, I didn't have time to worry about that as I had to get some things and hurry up and leave. Then I went into the girls' bedroom and took out my screwdriver to take the crib apart. I didn't know how I was going to get a crib on top of the Hyundai but God would help me figure out a way. In just under two hours, I took the crib apart, threw most of the girls' clothes in three plastic garbage bags, and hauled them out to the car. I started to panic because I knew it was getting close to the time Victor would be coming home for lunch. As I strapped the crib on top of the Hyundai with some rope I had, a woman stepped out of the house right next door.

"Can I help you?" she said.

I had been so busy packing up the car that I stared at her for a few seconds. Then I turned around and looked up and down the block — there were more people standing outside their houses watching me pack up the car! I stopped what I was doing and walked over to her.

"As a matter of fact, you could have helped me several months ago when my husband was beating the shit out of me. I knew you were home that morning and you heard me screaming for my life. You could have called the police. You also saw the Military Police come to my house. You knew I was pregnant and you could have helped me but you didn't." She lowered her eyes in shame.

"I didn't want to get involved," she said quietly.

I hoped that what I said next would haunt her for the rest of her life.

"Well, because you didn't want to get involved, it ALMOST cost me my life and it DEFINITELY cost my daughter her life!"

She turned and walked away from me, went inside her house and closed the door. Time was slipping by quickly, so I went back to packing up the car as I only had forty-five minutes left. After I was done, I got into the car and headed over to Tracey's house. Harry knew I was going to be there and Tracey asked him not to tell Victor I was there. She was happy to see me and hugged me as soon as I got out of the car.

"Gurl, you did it!" she said.

"Yep and I'm finally glad to be gone!" I replied.

We sat and talked for a few hours before I realized it was late and needed to get some sleep for the drive back later that night. When my head hit the pillow, I fell asleep instantly, knowing that I was finally free from Victor and it was the first good sleep I've had in months.

When I woke up, Tracey was kind enough to have fixed me some food to take on the road with me. I was ever so thankful for that, because I didn't have much money. I quickly washed my face, grabbed my bag and headed out the door.

"Gurl, you be safe on the road," she said as she walked me out the door.

As I got closer to the car, I realized something was not right. The bags inside the car looked as if someone had rifled through them. I stood there thinking, with my hands on my hips, before it hit me. Victor knew I was at Tracey's house! He had gone through the car at some point and removed some articles of my clothing and pictures of the girls. I couldn't care less because I was leaving North Carolina for good. Just as I was about to breathe a sigh of relief that I had been successful in getting out of North Carolina without incident, Victor appears out of the darkness. He had someone drive him there and drop him off.

Shit!!!! What is this, a game of cat and mouse? I thought as Victor walked up to me.

"Hi Ivette, I knew you would be here!" Victor said, matter-of-factly.

I figured I'd confront him about what he took out the car.

"Victor, you took some stuff out of the car that belonged to me!" I said.

"No, some of that stuff was actually mine because I paid for it!" he replied back.

I walked past Victor towards the car, determined not to have a confrontation with him.

"Ivette, I don't have any transportation. Could you drop me off at home?" Victor asked sheepishly.

"I don't have time for you or your games Victor. Whoever it was that dropped you off, they can pick you up!"

"Please Ivette, I promise I won't talk to you. I just need a ride," he said.

I turned what he said over in my mind. He knew he couldn't talk me into coming back to him because it was clear I wasn't going to. How much damage could a ride do? I thought to myself.

"Ok, I'll give you a ride. The moment you open your mouth, you're on the side of the road."

I kissed and hugged Tracey goodbye as Victor got into the car.

Tracey said under her breath, "Gurl, I don't trust him. You'd better be safe!"

"I will, Tracey. Don't worry, I'll be just fine and I'll call you when I get back to New York."

True to his word, Victor didn't say anything. I said nothing as well as I hurried up and drove him to the house on Spear Drive.

"Do you want to come inside for something to drink?" Victor asked as I pulled the car into a parking spot across the street from the house.

"Nope, gotta go!" I said. I was getting ready to pull the car into gear.

"Don't you want to wait at least until I get into the house safely?"

Then he looked towards the house with a puzzled look on his face.

"Wait a minute! I didn't leave the lights on in the living room! Ivette, you wait here while I go and check it out!" Victor exclaimed.

"I don't have time for your shit Victor!" I yelled out the car window as he ran across the street into the house.

Curiosity got the better of me as I stayed for a few seconds to see how this game would play out. I watched as Victor slowly walked up the stairs to the front door of the house. Then, he kicked the door open and lunged forward as if he was being pulled into the living room by some unseen force. What I saw next was beyond my imagination. Victor stood up and swung at someone but there was no one there! Then, he leaped onto where the couch was and I could see his arms moving up and down as if he was fighting someone. Victor shadowboxed for a few more minutes before he ran out of the house and back to the car, clearly out of breath.

"Ivette, someone was in the house!" he said, huffing and puffing.

"Mighty funny someone would be in the house when you come back to North Carolina! Stay here while I call the police because you are a witness!"

I couldn't contain myself anymore and burst out laughing as I put the car into gear and drove away. I laughed so hard I could barely see the road because of the tears in my eyes. I had seen it all! First he hit himself in the head with the hammer to frame me, now this!

I got back on the road to New York to put as much distance between me and Victor as I could. Victor wasn't going to drag me into any more of his games! By the time I got back to New York and into the house, my mother told me that Victor called several times while I was away. Before I left, I told my mother why I was going back there and that I would be staying at Tracey's house. By her telling Victor I wasn't there, I guess he figured out the rest.

The more time went by, the more Victor called my mother's house to harass me about coming back to him. He refused to believe that I was finally standing my ground on this. When I asked Victor for money because the girls went through ninety-six diapers a week, he would send me post-dated checks. Then I remembered the Basic Allowance for Quarters that he received and had to send to his family if we were not living with him. I had no other choice but to call Ft. Bragg and find out how I could start receiving the money and wanted to make sure that he didn't cheat me out of it like he did the last time because it was for his daughters. In order to get the BAQ started, I needed to speak to his

Company Commander to let him know I was no longer living on base. When Victor found out that I called his Company Commander, he became more determined to make my life even more miserable in New York. Then, without warning, without so much as a phone call, he just showed up at my mother's house one day for a "visitation" with the girls and said he wanted to talk to me. He hadn't seen Victoria and Yolanda since I left almost a year prior!

When my mother let him in and she walked towards the back of the house, again I told Victor the girls needed diapers. He just shrugged his shoulders.

"I've got twenty-five dollars in my pocket and I'm going to the department store to buy some gloves for myself," he told me.

I wasn't going to deal with this again so I asked my mother for a few dollars to get the girls some diapers right in front of him. Victor was so incensed when I did that that he waited until I was out of my mother's eyesight when he attacked me in my mother's house! He tried to put me in the same combat chokehold he did when I was pregnant with the twins. But this time, I fought him back. He underestimated me and assumed that I couldn't defend myself because my shoulder was broken from the last assault. As we struggled, I got so angry that it scared me because I don't believe I've ever been that angry before.

Oh, no, not again! Thismothafuckinbootlickinfatiguewearinbastard has the nerve to assault me in my mother's house!" I frantically thought.

Then with all my strength and as his hand was passed my mouth to complete the chokehold, I clamped down on him as hard with my teeth as hard as I could and wasn't going to let him go until he let me go, even if that meant drawing blood!

"Ahhhhhhhhhhhhhhhhhhhhh!" Victor screamed as loud as he could.

Then he let me go as he grabbed his hand and started jumping up and down from the pain. My mother came running down the hallway because she heard him screaming and Victoria ran ahead of her.

"Leave my mommy alone! Let my mommy go!" Victoria screamed as she repeatedly hit Victor on his legs.

"What happened?" my mother yelled. Then Victor started huffing and puffing like an idiot.

"Ivette just went crazy, attacked me and bit me for no reason! I just wanted to talk to her!" Victor yelled. Was he for real?

He seemed to ignore the fact that Victoria was still hitting him. I stood there with fire and brimstone in my eyes. I was the one that was huffing and puffing! I thought to myself that if he puts his hands on me again, I'll give him more where that came from!

Just like clockwork, my mother jumped to his defense.

"Ivette, what in the world is wrong with you? What did you do that for?"

I just rolled my eyes at her and said nothing. I took Victoria and went in my bedroom. I had had enough of all of this. I wasn't even safe in my own mother's house!

"Victor, you're going to have to leave now," I heard my mother say.

Victor said something indignant and left her house. I didn't bother to call the police although, in thinking about it now, I should have.

I went to work the next day trying to forget about Victor attacking me again. When I got home, I got as far as the front steps when I noticed Victor and a police officer walking towards me. I stood on the steps of my building and waited.

"Are you Ivette Wilson?" the officer asked.

"Yes," I said as I noticed Victor standing there with a smile on his face.

"This is a summons to appear in Court for denial of visitation and a Restraining Order. If you fail to appear in Court, a judgment will be entered against you and your children will be taken from you."

I couldn't believe that this bastard attacked ME and ended up getting a Restraining Order! (Fig. 1)

"If I don't work, I don't get paid officer. What am I supposed to do?" I said.

"I don't have anything to do with that. You just have to appear in Court," the officer said.

After I snatched the papers from the officer, he shook Victor's hand and walked off.

"Punk ass little bitch!" I mumbled under my breath. Here we go again with the war games!

When I went to court the following day and appeared in front of Judge Bruce M. Kaplan, I filed a counterclaim that Victor assaulted me and that I wanted a Restraining Order as well. He read my complaint, he mentioned that he saw my husband the day before and let me know he was not happy about me "assaulting" a distinguished member of the Armed Forces. As I tried to explain to the judge what happened, he chastised me as if I was the kid with the hand caught in the cookie jar. Even some twenty years later, I can still remember what Judge Kaplan said to me in Court.

"I saw Sergeant Wilson yesterday. You've done nothing but make trouble for a man serving his country and all he wants to do is see his children!!"

"But your Honor…," I started, when he cut me off.

"I saw the bite mark!" he yelled. I still tried to tell my side of the story.

"Your Honor, he started choking me in my mother's home!" I said anyway.

As he looked down and started to write something, it was clear to me that he was clearly annoyed.

"I'm going to issue you a Restraining Order; not because you need one, but only because you're entitled to one."

What made this Judge think I didn't need protection from someone with military training, a history of abuse and easy access to guns? How could this Judge not wonder what position Victor was in in order for his hand to be near my mouth and be bitten? Would anyone in their right mind think that he would stand there while I put his hand in my mouth to bite him?

From 1989 to about 1991, Victor used the Family Court system and child welfare agencies to not only maintain his power and control over me, but he even went so far as to use my daughters as a way to punish me for leaving him. Anyone within the court system that I spoke to about the abuse treated me with indifference. It was all in vain because the Courts believed everything Victor told them and even accused me of causing trouble for him when all I tried to do was make sure that my girls and I were safe and our rights were protected. As a result of the

Court's actions, not only did they not factor in the abuse when they made their decisions, but they continued to put my daughters and me in harm's way by allowing Victor unrestrained access to us. I was even told by Judge Kaplan to give him what he wanted since he was only visiting for a few days! Because Victor knew that I made an hourly wage and didn't get paid for the days I didn't work, he tried to financially bankrupt me by forcing me into Court so I wouldn't get paid. In his sick and twisted mind, if I couldn't work, I would be completely dependent on him and would have no other choice but to go back to him.

According to the Court, Victor had to give me a week's notice before he came to pick up the girls. But there were times when Victor came to New York and didn't tell me; instead, he would just show up at my mother's door to set me up for yet another Court appearance. One example was when he came to my mother's house unannounced and asked to see the girls at 11:00 p.m.

"Victor, the girls are asleep. You were supposed to give me a week's notice. You didn't call me."

He stormed away and the next day, I was served with papers to appear in Court for violating the Restraining Order and interfering with his visitation rights. When I went to Court, I took a notarized letter to prove to the Judge that he was abusive. The Judge refused to accept my letters and they never made it into my Court file.

After all the back and forth in Court, Judge Kaplan assigned a forensic evaluator by the name of Marcia Werchol, M.D. to our case to determine the state of our mental health. After my interview with her, this was the report she submitted to the judge.

> *Excerpt from Clinical Report*
> *ADJ. DATE 12/18/89*
> *Clinician: Marcia Werchol, M.D.*
> *Identification and issue*
>   *Ms. [name withheld] is the 23 year old respondent mother in these visitation proceedings concerning subject children [Girl 1] and [Girl 2]. There had been a series of petitions and counter-petitions since initiation of the proceedings by her estranged husband [name withheld], in*

July 1989; as of the most recent previous adjournment date 9/22/89, each party had been granted a temporary Order of Protection against the other, and Mr. [name withheld] had been granted a temporary Order of Visitation, stipulating day-time visitation of six hours duration, to be scheduled, according to his availability and notification of Ms. [name withheld], one week in advance.

CLINIC INTERVIEW

Ms. [name withheld] was interviewed at MHS by the undersigned for approximately one and three quarter hours. She was an articulate and superficially cooperative informant, but remained tense and distant throughout the interview. Furthermore, she was overwhelmingly pre-occupied by her resentment and rage toward her estranged husband, as a result of which her account was quite subjective.

She reported herself to have been born and raised in New York, the older of two children of parents who had divorced when she was 17 or 18; three older siblings by her mother's first marriage also had resided in the household. Her mother's first marriage had ended in divorce as a result of abandonment by the husband, that with the respondent's father as a result of his extra-marital affairs. Although the estrangement between her parents had begun when she was 8 or 9, she denied having observed frequent overt conflict between them and emphasized that there had been no physical violence or abuse in the home, though corporal punishment had sometimes been practiced.

Both parents had been employed, the mother as a geriatric psychiatry nurses' aide, now retired, the father as a chef, still working. The respondent indicated a closer relationship with her mother, who had been the primary caretaker and was described as being a quiet, somewhat reserved but also somewhat strong-willed woman. While she stated that she bears no resentment towards her father, she acknowledged that she has become distant from him and noted that he had always been rather unavailable, due to work on social involvements, and inclined to make many unfulfilled promises. She and her younger sister were said to have been and remain exceptionally close, although they had frequently fought as children. Her relationships with her two half-sisters were also reported to be close, but that with her half-brother to be distant, due to his having been incarcerated for reasons unknown to her during her childhood. She noted that her half-brother, a former substance abuser, had continued to do poorly, he was unable to manage independently and sometimes residing in his mother's or sisters households, but often leaving as a result of arguments or his stealing. The remainder of the siblings were said to be doing well, all employed, two married with no children, and one separated with one child.

Ms. [name withheld] described herself as having been a particularly well-behaved, quiet child, without conspicuous disciplinary problems at home or school. Though somewhat isolated and not particularly popular, she reported she had maintained two or three close friendships throughout school and since. Her husband, whom she began dating at age 16, was her first boyfriend. Her academic performance in earlier grades was indicated to have been above average, she having been in "s.p." classes and passed the entrance exam to Brooklyn Technical High School. However, following her enrollment at the latter, her performance was mediocre, as she found the technical subjects difficult, although she did graduate. Thereafter, she indicated, she had been employed fairly constantly, except when precluded from so doing by pregnancy or child-care obligations, in the field of computers, including presently in data-entry.

She acknowledged a significant psychiatric history in that she had been hospitalized briefly for medical treatment following a serious suicide attempt, by overdose on her husband's medication precipitated by marital discord.

Thereafter, she had been involved in no formal psychotherapy or counseling, except for brief, unsuccessful marital counseling with her husband following the death of their younger child's twin. At present, she indicated no strong inclination towards therapy or counseling, as she feels that her mood and self-esteem have considerably improved simply by virtue of her no longer being involved in the marital situation, but she did not indicate a sense of opposition to becoming involved in some form of treatment. Medical history was non-contributory.

As noted above, she met her husband when they were both 16, following which they dated for three years until marrying in 1985. After the marriage, they were apart for one year, he having been in Military Service and stationed in the South, she remaining in New York with her mother and working. Within one year of her moving to the South, their first child, [name withheld] was born, followed in less than one year by the premature birth of twins, including [name withheld] and another daughter, who died shortly after birth. She initially separated from her husband and moved back to New York with her children about four months later when [name withheld] who had remained in the hospital for two months after birth, was well enough to travel.

After one month of separation, there was an attempt at reconciliation, Ms. [name withheld] returning to the South with her children, but after a short period, she again separated from her husband, since which time she and the children have resided in New York with her mother. Although Ms. [name withheld] stated she had initially experienced her husband as "nice and had deeply loved him", she acknowledged that the relationship had been conflicted from the beginning, there having been frequent arguments, particularly regarding expenses, and one physical confrontation, involving Ms. [name withheld] having punched her then – fiancée in the mouth when he failed to desist in "playfully" slapping her. During the courtship, there were other several other significant warning signs that the marriage would fail, including that Mr. [name withheld] had been under-involved in the planning of the wedding and had at one point abruptly called it off, and even after they had married, expressed, ambivalence about wife's joining him in the South. After she had joined him there, the problems in the relationship became more obvious and severe, including physical altercations.

Of these, the most prominent was physical conflict, which began within one week of her joining him and was initiated by her discovering of and confronting her husband with a letter from a former girl-friend, with whom he had apparently maintained a relationship even after the wedding. Thereafter, the violence continued on a regular basis and with worsening severity, ultimately culminating in an altercation as a result of which, Ms. [name withheld] alleged, she had gone into premature labor with the twins. Although she acknowledged actively participating in the altercations, she indicated that it was always her husband who initiated physical conflict, and while she also acknowledged having sometimes provoked such incidents, she considered the provocations generally to have been quite minor and unintentional. A major source of conflict was disagreement over finances, Ms. [name withheld] portraying her husband as having been preoccupied with money, materialistic, selfish and unwilling to uphold her share of the financial burden. She also accused him of having failed to fulfill other social obligations, he having been away from home, in her estimation, more than necessary, and essentially neglecting her and later, their children, such that se, although also working outside the home, had been primarily responsible for maintaining the household. Throughout he account, Ms. [name withheld] with an unvarying tone of resentment, faulted her husband for the failures in their relationship, while portraying herself, despite minimal avowal of provocative behavior on her part, as generally blameless and victimized, yet was unable to articulate why she had chosen to remain in so painful a situation for so long with only limited and possibly somewhat inappropriate attempts at seeking outside assistance (by complaining to her mother and superior officers), other than that she had loved her husband, had not wanted to involve others, and thus, had striven to maintain the relationship by her own efforts. Since their final separation, she indicated, contact has been minimal but consistent in quality with the previous pattern, and she has no inclination to reconcile with her husband, although he has made overtures in this regard.

At present Ms. [name withheld] indicated, both children are doing well and are at age-appropriate developmental levels, the younger, despite initial developmental lag, having rapidly caught up. Initially, she acknowledged, she had been somewhat overwhelmed b the responsibility of caring for two children so close in age, and had felt quite emotionally stressed as a result, but she denied that she had ever lost control with them. At present, she indicated them to present no particular management problems, not to require more discipline than occasional verbal admonishment or a light spanking.

During the day, while she works, they are cared for by her mother, in whose caretaking abilities she indicated full confidence. In contrast, she expressed very little confidence in the ability of her husband to care for the children, in that, she alleged, he had assumed no direct responsibility for the children prior to the separation nor had he indicated much interest in them. Indeed, she stated, to begin with he had been disinclined to have children, especially females and had been nearly distraught, according to Ms. [name withheld] description, when informed that her second pregnancy would result in multiple=birth, which reaction she attributed in part to his financial preoccupations. However, she acknowledged that it had been her husband who had given consent to blood transfusions for the twins at birth, which she declined to do because she is a Jehovah's Witness, and she further acknowledged that since the separation, he has been somewhat more attentive to the children, though she complained of his showing an unfair preference for the older child, and she insinuated that his increased attention to the children is, in any case, motivated more by his desire to maintain contact with her. Since the onset of formal visitation, contacts between the father and children have apparently gone well, the children subsequently showing no distress and seeming to have been adequately cared for, but Ms. [name withheld] continued to express reluctance in regard to the father's unsupervised visitation, particularly were it to be extended in duration, as she considered him to be insufficiently experienced or cautious. Furthermore, she feared that he might be inclined to act out his conflict with her through the children in some way, possibly by absconding with them, which action she stated, he had threatened in the past but admittedly had never acted upon.

Her concerns were no mitigated by the potential availability of the paternal grandmother as a direct or indirect supervisor, inasmuch as she experienced the paternal grandmother to be in complete ideological alignment with her son and therefore, disposed to collude in any harmful actions he might contemplate. However, she was unable to articulate any concrete basis for her concerns regarding either the father or paternal grandmother, and he opposition to visitation impressed as being primarily an outgrowth of her own anger toward the father.

MENTAL STATUS EXAMINATION

Ms. [name withheld] presented as an attractive, exquisitely groomed female appearing her stated age, and in fair physical health. Psychomotor behavior was socially appropriate, though somewhat tense. Speech was clear, coherent, logical and mostly relevant, but somewhat pressured and inclined to over-elaboration of her grievances regarding her estranged husband. Mood was depressed and angry, affect mostly constricted, except for acute and apparently genuine tearfulness when she spoke of the death of the other twin. There was no indication of formal thought disorder, delusions, or hallucinations, although she was markedly preoccupied with the conflict between her and her husband. Current suicidal and homicidal ideation was denied. Insight was limited to the extent of her being able to acknowledge herself "not perfect" and also acknowledge some obliviousness on her part regarding the instability of the marriage early on; otherwise, she accepted little accountability for her role in the conflicted relationship and tended to externalize blame. She impressed as being genuinely devoted to her children and having some empathy for them, but her empathic capacity was also indicated to be impaired by her subjective preoccupation regarding the father. Judgment impressed as generally intact, though as vulnerable to the same subjective distortion. No organic deficits were elicited, and intellectual functioning was assessed as being above average.

DIAGNOSTIC IMPRESSION

Axis I. – 300.40 Dysthymic Disorder (provisional)

Axis II. – Borderline Personality Features

Axis III. – No diagnosis

SUMMARY AND CONCLUSIONS

On the basis of past history and current presentation, Ms. [name withheld] is indicated to be a generally well-functioning individual, including as regards to the caretaking of her children. However, she also impresses as currently embittered, enraged and depressed, which emotional state would appear to be the result of a combination of chronic characterological features, and a more acute mood disturbance. This has played a role both in her part and present interpersonal conflict with her husband,

which in turn appears to be the primary basis of her
reluctance in regard to his being granted reasonable
visitation. However, there is no indication that it otherwise
impairs her ability to parent her children in an effective and
nurturing manner.

RECOMMENDATIONS

It is recommended that Ms. [name withheld] engage
in individual psychotherapy, to assist her in working out her
chronic and more acute emotional conflicts.
It is also recommended that in the event Mr. [name
withheld] relocates permanently to New York, she engage
with him in couples counseling, not necessarily in order to
effect a marital reconciliation, but in order to prevent their
continuing to act out their interpersonal conflicts via their
children.

Please refer to the report on the petitioner – father,
[name withheld] for additional recommendations.
Signed by Marcia Werchol, M.D.
Psychiatrist

I told her about the abuse! How could she recommend that we go to couple's counseling! Needless to say, she diagnosed Victor as having "Narcissistic Personality Features."

One day, while at Court, the law guardian for the children told me of a conversation she had had with Victor.

"Your husband seems to fear for the safety of his children because you're mentally unstable. You tried to commit suicide years earlier and he's worried for their safety."

It was his mention of my attempted suicide that prompted the Court to have the New York Society for the Prevention of Cruelty to Children to investigate me. (See Fig. 2) Needless to say, the case was unfounded.

The law guardian continued.

"Has your husband ever hit or abused the children?" I saw exactly where she was going with her line of questioning. Yet again, I felt the need to mention the abuse.

"Does it count that he abused me while I was pregnant and assaulted me in front of my own children? Does it count if he assaulted me while I was six-and-a-half months' pregnant with twins, went into premature labor and one of them died?" To this day, I will never forget her response.

"None of that matters as long as he didn't hit or abuse them directly," she said matter-of-factly.

I was shocked. What was wrong with these people? Was I the only one thinking that if you expose children to violence and abuse, that you're emotionally and psychologically abusing them as well? It was becoming clear to me that no one in the Family Court system knew anything about the true nature of domestic violence or abuse.

In the eyes of the Court, nothing I said or did mattered. I didn't have the option of not going, because the police would either threaten to arrest me and take my girls from me or, if I didn't give in to Victor and the Courts, they would take the girls from both of us and put them into foster care.

Victor never resolved the issue of sending me money for the girls and because I could no longer live on his post-dated checks that I couldn't deposit for a week or more, I went to the Child Support Enforcement Unit for help. The Child Support Office responded some weeks later that they couldn't find him and he was no longer in the military, although I gave them his current mailing address and social security number! I took my letter and went back to the Child Support Enforcement Unit to explain to them that he was still in the military.

"That's impossible! I know he's still in the military!" I told the clerk at the office.

"I'm sorry ma'am, but we called the military finance department and they informed us he is no longer with the military."

Yet another day I had to take off from work without pay.

Some days later, I got a phone call from Victor.

"I told you you wouldn't get child support from me." Then he hung up.

Neither the Courts, nor the police, nor the military systems ever questioned Victor or his motives. The New York City Family Court system gave him the freedom to travel from North Carolina to New York to harass and stalk me. Victor was a desperate man grasping at any and every opportunity to manipulate me, even to the extent of using his own children as pawns. I had no protection or support from anyone — not my family, not the Court system, the police, or even the military.

In the midst of my numerous Court appearances, I tried to find an attorney to at least explain to me what my rights were. I couldn't figure out if I needed a civilian attorney because I lived in New York or a civilian attorney with knowledge of the military. When I contacted the Legal Aid Society, I was informed that it would take three months to see an attorney! I was only making five or six dollars an hour at that time as a temporary worker and couldn't afford an attorney. And based on the income guidelines for the Legal Aid Society, I made too much money which made me ineligible for their services.

Here I am in New York with my two girls, I've left my abuser and am now living in my mother's house making pennies an hour as a temp. I couldn't afford an attorney and the attorneys that I spoke to that offered free consultations were interested in taking my case until I mentioned that Victor was in the military. Of all the times I appeared in Court, not one person ever asked me if my daughters or I needed any sort of help — housing, financial, or otherwise. Victor's antics were putting me in a real financial predicament. While he lived on Fort Bragg rent free, he amused himself by watching me struggle financially with the girls.

After being in New York for a while, I realized I hadn't received my credit card statements and never called them to give them my new mailing address. When I called the company to give them my new mailing address, they informed me that my credit card that was over the limit. I told them that wasn't possible because I had never used it. They begged to differ. They asked me if I was the owner of the account and I told them "No." That's when they informed me that according to their records, I was the Owner of the credit card account and Victor was the Co-Applicant. A few minutes went by before I figured it out.

Back when Victor and I first married and moved to North Carolina, he wanted to get a joint credit card. He told me to put my information on the application where it said "Co-Applicant," then he would add his information later and mail the form. I never saw Victor fill out the application in front of me. What he did was take the application with my information on it, got another blank application and put my information under "Applicant" and his name as "Co-Applicant," then forged my signature. When I found them hidden in his dresser and realized he never told me he received them, I asked him about it.

"Victor, why didn't you tell me you got the credit cards?"

Victor responded, "What do you need a credit card for? You don't have a job! When you get a job, then you'll get your credit card. I'm not going to let you run up my credit!"

I never thought to cancel the credit card because I decided I wouldn't use it.

I missed Little Susan terribly and still couldn't make sense of her death and that made me feel powerless. I wanted something, anything that could help me understand why Victor assaulted me when I was pregnant.

When I gave birth to the twins, I remembered that the Military Police wanted to investigate Victor's assault on me and the death of my daughter. I felt strong enough emotionally that I could deal with an investigation, so I checked with Fort Hamilton to see if the statute of limitations had run out. They told me it hadn't. I went to Fort Hamilton in Brooklyn to start the investigation and gave my statement in April of 1989, hopeful that I could get justice for Little Susan and myself. Victor gave his statement in May of 1989. Below is my statement.

Sworn Statement taken at Ft. Hamilton Resident Agency

I, [Name Withheld], In Sep 87, my husband, SGT [Name Withheld], and I moved into quarters [Address Withheld] on Ft. Bragg, NC. Later, during the month, I learned that I was pregnant. My husband was not happy about this and wanted me to get an abortion. I refused because of my religious convictions. We would fight almost daily on this topic. During this time our fights never escalated past shoving and pushing. In Jan 88, while I was talking to my mother, she suggested that she take my oldest daughter since she was only eight months old and I was having a hard time caring and feeding for her due to the pregnancy and because I was still working full time. I talked to my husband about it and he was not happy about the idea.

During one of the last days in Feb 88, I once again approached my husband about my mother taking out daughter. We started arguing again. I was tired or arguing with him and tried to leave the bedroom. At this time he pushed me down on the bed and pinned my wrists so that I could not get up or hit him. My daughter, who was on the bed at the time, started crying, so my husband put her in her crib. I also got up to try to calm her down. While I was in the hallway, [Husband] started to push me into the wall and threatened to push me down the stairs. He finally stopped pushing me since it was getting late and needed to go to work. I went downstairs to get away from him. When he came downstairs, I proceeded to go back upstairs since I did not want to be around him. While upstairs, I got angrier and started to throw papers around. Finally I knocked over a small table next to the bed, which held our telephone and answering machine. My husband heard this and came upstairs. When he saw that the answering machine was on the ground he came after me. He pushed me around and then started to choke me with the crook of his right arm. He then whispered in my ear, "You can't breathe now, can you." I was starting to black out when he let me go. He then left for work.

Prior to going to work, he took my car keys, ID card and telephone from the house. I got my daughter dressed and walked to the nearest telephone booth and contacted the 1SG of his unit and informed him what had happened. I then contacted the MP Station. I walked back home and five minutes later the MPs came by. I wrote a statement on what had happened to me. While I was writing my statement, my husband came back home. He tried to come over to me but the NPs got in his way. After I finished my statement, the MPs stated that they would contact his first sergeant and suggest that [Husband] be removed from the house in order for us to cool down. Later on that day my husband came back to the house and he was escorted by another individual from his unit. At 1830 that day, I again went to the telephone booth and tried to contact my mother. I was unable to contact her and when I got back home my husband was there on the phone talking to my mother. I talked to my mother and related what had happened. During the conversation I mentioned that I was not feeling well and my mother suggested that I go to the hospital. [Husband] volunteered to take me. After I got off the phone, I waited approximately 45 minutes while my husband fixed himself dinner and watched a basketball game. He dropped me off at the hospital and gave me money for cab fare since he told me that he needed to go back to the company later on. While in the hospital, the doctor stated that I was going into labor and that they needed to admit me in order to stop the delivery.

The female doctor that examined me noticed bruises around my neck and shoulders and asked if this is the reason why I was delivering earlier than expected. I told her yes. During this time they had placed me on Demerol in order to stop me from going into labor. It took about 2 hours for my husband to pick up my daughter from the hospital and take her home. Later I discovered that they had contacted him and he refused to pick her up. [I was in the hospital for several days] and we had thought they stopped me from going into labor. Later on, I started having contractions again and this time they were unable to stop me from going into labor. I had one of my daughters prior to getting into the delivery room and the other one had to be delivered by C-section.

During the delivery I lost a large amount of blood, but refused a blood transfusion due to my religious convictions. After delivery the babies had to be taken to a civilian hospital since they did not have an intensive care unit in the hospital. I called my mother and asked her to come to North Carolina. I remember her getting there about 5 hours later, but was still too weak and affected by the medication to remember anything of significance while she was there that day. The next day I was informed by [Husband] that one of my daughters had died that day.

Later on, another female CPT talked to me and gave me information on support groups on parents who have lost children. She had read my records and knew that my husband assaulted me and related the he could be charged with assault on me and possibly charged with the murder of my child. Since I was still weak from the loss of blood and on medication at the time I did not want to deal with the situation. I left my husband in Jul 88 once the doctors stated that she was fit to travel. In Aug 88, I decided to give my husband another chance, against my best judgment.

When I arrived there, there was sill a lot of tension and I would stay away from the house whenever possible. In early Sep 88, we were driving to my girlfriends house so that I could visit her. While on the way [Husband] asked if I would co-sign a loan with him at the bank and open a joint account. I told him no. We argued about this even at my girlfriends house. Finally I told him that I did not want to fight anymore and that he should go and just let me stay at my girlfriends house. I went out to the car to get my purse. On the way back to the house he turned me around and tried to push me back to the car.

Finally he picked me up from underneath my arms and threw me to the ground. It felt like he had broken my shoulder since it hurt so much. The ambulance and police were called. The people at the ambulance placed a splint on my arm until I could go to the hospital. The civilian police arrived and both myself and my girlfriend provided them with verbal statements. After arriving at the hospital at Ft Bragg, we gave the MPs written statements on what had happened. The MPs took my husband down to the station and went back home. I stayed there for about three days and went back home. In Sep 88, I left my husband and came to New York and have lived with my mother ever since.

Q. Did anybody see or hear the fight that you had with your husband in Feb 88?

A. Yes a neighbor two doors down came over after the MPs left with my husband and asked if I needed help since she had heard me screaming.

Q. Do you know her name?

A. No, but looking at my quarters she lived in the second house on the right.

Q. Concerning the incident in Feb 88, did your husband hit you?

A. No.

Q. Did he kick you.

A. No he only pushed me and strangled me.

Q. At the hospital in Mar 88, who was the doctor who observed the bruises around your neck and shoulders?

A. I think it was Dr (CPT) Marianne Willie.

Q. Who was the female CPT who talked to you about the support group?

A. I do not remember.

Q. Prior to the incident in Feb 88, were there any complications in your pregnancy?

A. Just slight hemorrhaging during my third or fourth month.

Q. Prior to the incident, were you on any medication?

A. No

Q. How long have you and [Husband] been married?

A. Four years.

Q. Are you currently legally separated?
A. No
Q. Are you planning on divorce?
A. Yes
Q. During your pregnancy Had [Husband] ever hit you?
A. No
Q. Do you feel that the assault your husband committed on you is the reason why you prematurely went into labor?
A. Yes.
Q. Is there anything you wish to add or delete from this statement?
A. No.
Signed by me and by [name withheld], April 1, 1989, Investigator

I was told that in order to get a copy of Fort Hamilton's criminal investigation report under the Freedom of Information Act, I had to write to the Department of the Army in Falls Church, Virginia. Months later, I received a letter from the U.S. Army Crime Records Center:

> *...This is in reply to your Privacy Act request of August 9, 1989 for release of information pertaining to your husband, Sergeant Victor Wilson and supplements our letter of August 18, 1989.*
>
> *The enclosed U.S. Army Criminal Investigation Command (USACIDC) Preliminary Inquiry, which is responsive to your request, is part of a system of records that is exempt from the mandatory access provisions of the Privacy Act and the mandatory disclosure provisions of the Freedom of Information Act (FOIA). The portions of the report, which have been withheld, are denied to you because release of this information would disclose the identification number of our special agent, and violate the personal privacy of other individuals. It is important to note, that a preliminary inquiry means no formal criminal investigation was initiated because no evidence of criminality was discovered....*

It seemed that no matter where I turned to get justice, I was met with a brick wall. The letter also informed me that I could file for an appeal, but I quickly realized that this was going to be a long uphill battle and I still had to deal with Victor hauling me into Court on a whim.

In the meantime, I started receiving BAQ checks from the military which were deducted from Victor's check – all $387 of it for two children. I received that same amount of money from Victor without an increase for the next eighteen years. A few times I didn't receive the check and had to track it down to find out what happened. Since Victor and I weren't on good terms, I had no other choice but to call the Military Finance Office in Indianapolis to inquire about whether the money was taken out of his check. Once when I called the Finance Office, I was told it hadn't been taken out of his check and that I should call Victor's commanding officer to follow up. Once, it was lost in the mail, so I had to check with the post office. When I called his commanding officer and gave them my name, I was told he "wasn't there." So, that meant I had to call a few times until I spoke to him. Each time, I was told he wasn't there.

After not receiving a response from Victor's Company Commander, I wrote a letter to him instead and sent it certified mail, returned receipt to make sure he received my letter. Maybe Victor was trying to set me up, but following up with his Company Commander via letter after not receiving a response via phone did more damage than good.

Victor came to New York unannounced and had me served with another Violation of Order of Protection and a notice to appear in Court. He used my letter to his Company Commander as proof that I was "causing him undue harassment."

This drama with Victor and the Courts made me feel the same loneliness and isolation I felt while living in North Carolina. I didn't feel safe at my mother's house either, because she would always let Victor in then put in her two cents later that my children needed their father. Despite all that the girls and I went through, I also had to contend with my mother being angry at me for marrying Victor one minute and then for leaving him the next. It always bothered me that she never gave me credit for not only being strong enough to leave Victor, but strong enough to never go back.

To add insult to injury, Victor threatened to take my girls from me and said that I would never see them again. Part of me felt this was another one of his mind games and part of me felt that he would actually make good on his threats. It was a matter of time before my worst fears came true.

I came home from work one day, glad to finally be home and was looking forward to spending time with my girls. This particular day, they didn't meet me at the door to hug me like they've done countless times before. Right away, I had a sinking feeling in the pit of my stomach. I ran towards the living room where my mother sat and still no sign of Victoria and Yolanda.

"Where are the girls?" I asked my mother.

"Victor came by and took them. He said he talked to you and you said it was okay."

All the color drain from my face.

"Are you kidding me? You yourself said Victor was a liar and you didn't think to call me and see if that was true? I never spoke to Victor, Ma. He never called me!" I screamed. Her face went blank.

The next thing I did was call Susan.

"Susan, it's Ivette. Did Victor come to New York? Is he there?" I asked.

"No, he's not here," she responded.

I got frustrated and hung up the phone. I knew she was lying! I couldn't think straight because my mind raced a mile a minute. My God, Victor kidnapped my girls and I didn't know where they were! Since Victor and I were separated but legally married, what he did wasn't considered kidnapping. I didn't know what I would do if anything happened to them. Moreover, I was furious with my mother for trusting Victor and letting him take the girls and I really didn't want to speak to her. Several hours later, my mother's phone rang. It was Victor.

"I promised you I would take the girls! I told you that I could take them back to North Carolina and you would never see them again!"

"You bring my daughters back to me!" I yelled.

All of a sudden, his mother broke into the conversation, her voice sounding sad.

"If you want them home, then I'll send them home."

I took a few seconds for everything to register in my mind. Victor called me from his mother's house! I KNEW she was lying to me about Victor being in New York! Not only did she know where they were all along, she was listening to the whole conversation from the other phone in their house!

Victor eventually bought the girls back home, none the wiser that they had were used as innocent pawns in Victor's game of power and control. Once they got into the house, I slammed the door in Victor's face. I was never so glad to see my girls!

Victor's games continued for quite some time where he would come to New York unannounced and then take me to Court for violating the Order of Protection although I neither saw nor spoke to him. I realized this visitation battle wasn't for him; it was so his mother could see the girls.

In December 1989, Judge Ruth Jane Zuckerman took over my case and did nothing different than what Judge Kaplan did. They both put my children and me in harm's way by allowing Victor not only liberal access to them, but to me as well. (See Fig. 3) Victor didn't care about what the court said or about the children; he only did this to make my life miserable.

Although I complied with everything the Courts required of me, including cooperating with Society for the Prevention of Cruelty to Children (SPCC), I found it perplexing that both judges granted Victor liberal visitation rights when he didn't comply with the investigation from SPCC.

Just a note: In 2009 while completing my research for this book, I went to the New York Family Court to obtain a copy of my file. To my surprise, there were documents in the file that I never knew about. For years, I could not understand why the Courts perceived me as a someone who was making trouble for an active duty service member. Although I remembered trying to get Judge Kaplan to look at my notarized letters, he never accepted them and they never made it in my file. I did, however, find an undated letter from his Company Commander that Victor gave to the Judge which when I read it, explained why the Court treated my case the way they did. (See Fig. 4)

Chapter 20

Winter 1989 — Free At Last

In the middle of our court battle, Victor and I divorced in 1989. Because he involved the court system to keep control over me, now they were going to be in our lives until Victoria and Yolanda turned eighteen. There would always be the constant threat hanging over my head that he could haul me into court anytime he couldn't get what he wanted.

So far, he had been successful in portraying me in the courts as the "evil" mother alienating him from his kids. He knew I couldn't afford an attorney to represent me in family court and he also knew I couldn't afford an attorney to divorce him, so he "offered" to pay for the divorce. As his bargaining chip, he agreed that he would give me full custody if I "just signed" the papers. Why would a father that "loved" his children so much just give up custody? At one time, Victor asked me how much I wanted in child support and told him I would get back to him. His exact words were that he "wanted the best for his daughters and he wanted them to go to private school." Therefore, I sat down and figured out how much I spent on the girls: ninety-six diapers a week, food and clothing, as well as day care expenses and came up with the amount of six hundred dollars. When I got back to him and told him the amount, he went ballistic.

"You must be outta your fucking mind if you think I'm going to give you six hundred dollars! I'm not going to screw myself like that!"

"But I thought you wanted the best for your kids," I said back to him.

As he continued his tirade, I interrupted him and told him to send me the papers. Then I hung up.

I was tired of this back and forth game with Victor. I just wanted my freedom and I would deal with everything that came afterwards. Victor relinquished custody with no provisions for child support and I signed them. I was happy to finally be divorced and he was happy with visitation rights.

I frequently wondered how this would affect Yolanda and Victoria as they got older. Would witnessing the abuse make them vulnerable to being abused or make them abusers? How would all of this affect them psychologically? One thing was for sure, it had a noticeable effect on Victoria. She developed a nervous habit of banging her head on the bed from seeing Victor assault me on numerous occasions. Yolanda, on the other hand, was spared because I left when she was still an infant. I felt helpless because I couldn't protect them from being constantly disappointed by Victor or being used as pawns by him. It also bothered me that Yolanda will always feel that a part of her is missing because of Little Susan's death.

To make matters worse, Yolanda needed to be tested for AIDS after having a blood transfusion at birth. AIDS was beginning to rear its ugly head at the time and the Army always encouraged their enlisted to donate blood. I remember a news broadcast when I lived in North Carolina that the military was not testing donated blood, so several people contracted AIDS as a result. She was about three when I had her tested and, thank God, the test came out negative. Although Yolanda was small for her age and she was hospitalized on a few occasions for asthma and upper respiratory infections, she was doing well. Being born at twenty-six weeks, she could have developed far worse health issues, such as going blind from her exposure in the oxygen tent or being developmentally disabled from an underdeveloped brain.

On one of Victor's visits to take the girls out, Yolanda happily went with him but Victoria didn't want to go. She cried and screamed if I tried to make her. She had already been through enough and I didn't want to traumatize her further, so I never made her go. I always held out hope that as long as I taught them the difference between right from wrong, that they would eventually see Victor for what he was and I was right. As Victor picked up Yolanda, Victoria grabbed my leg and wouldn't let go.

"I'll give you candy if you go with me," Victor would say.

"My mommy can buy me candy," Victoria said back. Although she was only five years old, I knew she couldn't be bought with trinkets.

"I'll buy you a toy if you go with me," Victor said.

"My mommy can buy me toys," Victoria sassed back. I felt Victor was sending the wrong message to the girls and I let him know that.

"Victor, you are not teaching them anything. If you're supposed to be their father, they will want to spend time with you because they want to, not because you buy them things. What are you going to do when the toys get bigger and more expensive? What will you do then? You can't buy their love to make up for the fact that you're not around!" I said to him.

"Leave me alone! I'll do with MY daughters what I want to do!" he snapped at me.

He always acted as if the girls were mere possessions to him, not human beings with feelings, thoughts and emotions.

"Okay, but remember it's not MY responsibility to make sure you have a relationship with them. That's YOUR job and however that relationship is going to turn out, it will be your own doing." I told Victor.

In the hopes of strengthening my faith to help me through all of this, I started going back to the Kingdom Hall again. Being re-victimized by Victor and the family court system had a profound effect on me. I still grieved for Little Susan, my mother constantly interfered with how I raised my daughters and she showed her lack of support and understanding by verbally beating me down at every turn. Since I wasn't in the financial position to get my own apartment and, with only a high school education, my job prospects were limited.

Because of my mother, now everyone in the Kingdom Hall knew about what happened to me and that I lost my daughter. And with knowing that, they still continued to treat me and my daughters as if we had the plague. I tried to ignore the very people that watched me and my sister grow up ignore me as I attended the Kingdom Hall on a weekly basis. I held my head up high and decided I no longer cared what anyone thought of me. One night after service, one of the elders approached me.

"Hey, Ivette, how have you been? I haven't seen you at service in a while."

For a brief moment, I felt that someone actually cared enough to want to know how I was feeling.

"Elder, I've been going through a lot lately. I'm still dealing with the death of my daughter and now my husband is trying to take my children away from me."

"Well I'm glad to see that you're attending Kingdom Hall again. But you know, everything that's happening to you including your daughter's death, is your punishment for your sins. You know the "Truth" and what the Bible says about non-believers and people of the world and yet you married someone who was a non-believer."

My mouth fell open! My first inclination was to slug him right there! How DARE he say that to me! How DARE he judge me! I knew he didn't have any children of his own, so how could he know what it was like to lose a child! I felt victimized all over again. I grabbed my girls and left, extremely disappointed and disillusioned because I had grown up as a Jehovah's Witness in that very congregation. Everyone knew my family and me. How could he say such a thing! As I traveled back home, I turned over and over in my mind what that Elder said. I became more confused between what I learned as a Jehovah's Witness growing up and how I was being treated by people in my congregation. I was raised in a religion that preached "love thy neighbor as thyself," yet they would walk past me and not speak. I began to realize how hypocritical they were and that was when I began to question whether that religion was the right one for me. Thoughts screamed through my mind and bounced back and forth in my head like a ping pong ball.

God is a God of love!

No He isn't if He is punishing you for your sins!

God wouldn't allow me to come this far just to punish me some more!

I was a good Christian wife! I did everything the Bible said!

No you weren't! Everything happened because you didn't listen to your husband!

But I listened to my husband and now my daughter is dead!

You should have never married him because he is not a Jehovah's Witness!

How are Witnesses better! I know some who have hit their wives!

At twenty-three years of age, I concluded that being a Jehovah's Witness was not the religion for me after all. In fact, any organized religion that will not allow me to think for myself is not the religion for me. I've learned that there is a BIG difference between religion and spirituality.

Religion is something you "do." It dictates that the only path to God and Salvation is by practicing an organized set of rules and obeying them without question. Religion instills fear in that if you don't practice these organized rules, that you will not have God's favor. Religion is the "middle man" between a person and God. However, along that path, religious teachings are distorted and when it is applied in a negative way, can shatter a person's belief system.

Spirituality is something you "have within you." It refers to an individual's personal path to God or a Higher Power. Spirituality focuses on getting to know your True Self and nurturing your Inner Spirit to be in harmony with that Higher Power.

Since that experience, I have not been back to that Kingdom Hall or any Kingdom Hall for that matter. Although I have maintained my faith in a Higher Power, I realized that I didn't need a "middle man" or be in a physical Kingdom Hall to prove that I believed in Him. God knows all and sees all and more importantly, He knows what is in my heart. After all, it was my faith in my Higher Power that helped me survive this in the first place. Being a Jehovah's Witness meant the ability to make decisions for myself being stripped away through fear and intimidation and I had had enough of that from Victor and my mother.

I was tired of trying to please my mother, my husband, people in the Kingdom Hall, even the courts. I always tried to do the right thing and tell the truth because that was how I was raised. While everyone entertained themselves by watching me bend over backwards to please them, I was miserable because I didn't get anything out of this for myself. I wasn't allowed to further my education when I wanted to because of how I was raised and what the Kingdom Hall taught, but instead was groomed to get married, have kids and take care of my husband. I had to learn how to play "catch up" with my own life. I eventually learned to block out all the physical, emotional and verbal abuse because I was conditioned to think that no one would believe me if I told them. That coping mechanism ended up doing more harm than good. What it did was put me in a state of "autopilot" where I focused my attention on what I needed to do for the day so I didn't have time to think about all the horrible things that happened.

I felt like a hamster in a wheel, constantly going around and around, yet going nowhere. I wanted the same things most people want out of life. I wanted to be happy, violence-free, have my own apartment and, more importantly, I wanted to raise my girls without interference from Victor, my mother, the Kingdom Hall or the courts.

After my encounters with Victor and the court appearances became far and few in between, I started dating and that caused several arguments between my mother and me.

"Those girls need a father," she would say.

"Not if he's going to continue to abuse me! Instead of you always blaming me for leaving Victor, did it ever occur to you to be glad that I had the sense to leave him?" I said back to her.

Why didn't someone blame Victor for what he did or hold him responsible for his own actions? I didn't MAKE him abuse me! I thought about how people reacted to what I went through — from my next door neighbor in North Carolina who didn't want to get involved, to my mother telling me my place was with my husband, to a religion that basically condoned abusive behavior. Not once did anyone say to me, "Ivette, you don't have to die, I'll take your place," or "Ivette, you don't deserve to be abused; you deserve so much better." But let me try to have a little happiness in my life and someone will always be ready to take THAT from me! When I stopped listening to what people had to say is when I became the "black sheep" of my family.

I took control of my life by designating some "mommy" time for myself — just a few hours a week where I would ask my mother to watch the girls to go dancing at the club. Because I met Victor when I was sixteen, I never had the chance to date anyone else or learn about the "Dating Game." I had several reasons for wanting to go out. First, I wanted to be around people my own age in a social setting. Two, if I wanted to date, I would never meet anyone by staying at home. Third, listening to the music pound in my ears for a few hours helped me forget about everything that troubled me. When I did date, I was always careful not to involve my daughters in my relationships and to keep the two separate. It seemed the more I went out and socialized, the less I thought about what I went through with Victor.

Two years after I got my divorce from Victor, I got the shock of my life — my father passed away from cancer.

Two days before my father died, I took my Victoria and Yolanda to see him. By then, he had left my mother and moved in with another woman who was living in the Bronx. For as long as I live, I will always remember those few precious hours I spent with him. He loved having his granddaughters around him and made no bones about telling them he loved them whenever he got the chance, just like he did when I was a child. Moreover, as long as they were with their Grandpa, there was nothing I could say to them — he would tell me to "leave his babies alone. They can have whatever they want." Back then, I could see that there was a rare and special bond between my girls and their Grandpa.

I will always believe that a father holds a special place in a young girl's life. He is her first encounter with someone of the opposite sex and how that relationship develops will determine what kind of men she will have relationships with when she gets older. While my mother was the disciplinarian of the family, with her "my way or the highway" attitude about things, my father was more laid back. There were stark differences between my parents and I wondered how they got married in the first place. My mother's way of saying "I Love You," was "If I didn't love you, I would do this, or that." My father's way of saying "I Love You," was to just come out and say it. And, I will always remember my father never being afraid to tell us how much he loved us.

While I sat and talked with him while he played with the girls, I noticed he didn't look well. For fear of jinxing the situation, I said nothing. As a kid, you believe that your parents will live forever, and the thought of them dying never occurs to you. It definitely didn't occur to me, even at the age of twenty-five. In the middle of talking to the girls, he said to me, "Vettie, always remember I love you and never let anyone hurt you. I want you, Bernice and your brothers to stay in contact with each other and stay together." I was surprised that my father would say that because he always lived for the moment and I respected him because of that. I wanted to say to him, "Daddy you're talking like you're going somewhere," but again, I didn't want to jinx anything. He also told me that he loved my mother and he couldn't understand why she was so mean to him. I remember times when I was a kid that my parents argued and I even remember times when my mother hit my father hard enough to draw blood. Despite all of that, he could still say that he loved her. I always felt that I was more like him than my mother. He was the type of person that everyone liked, and although he had a drinking problem and cheated on my mother, he was never abusive to us. Despite his faults, he was my father and I loved him dearly.

When it was time for the girls and me to go home, I hugged my father and said I would see him later. I didn't want to say goodbye to him as I struggled to hold back the tears because I knew, deep down inside, I would never see him again.

The next day, I received a phone call from his new wife that he was in the hospital due to difficulties he had the night before with his breathing. I told her that I would come and see him and she asked that I give him the night to rest and I could visit him the next day. I gave her the number to the day care center to call me if there was any change in his condition. The following day, as I dropped the girls off at the day care center, I received a phone call. It was his wife and she told me he was gone.

Chapter 21

Winter 1990 — Freedom

After working as an office temporary for a couple of years, I landed a job working for the City and was able to save enough money to move out of my mother's house. I also registered at Bronx Community College and took classes at night to become a Systems Analyst. When I moved out, I arranged with my mother to watch the girls during the week while I worked and went to class and I would have them on the weekends. Then I found a one-bedroom apartment in the Bronx for five hundred and fifty dollars a month shortly after my father passed away. At that time, I didn't have much time to date because I worked during the day and went to school at night.

When I think about the few guys I was able to date with my busy schedule, there was only one that that made a life-long impression on me. Mark* and I attended the same high school and we casually dated for about nine months. He was a nice person who treated me different from anyone I had been with, including Victor, because he treated me like a lady in private as well as in public. It was my first taste of a healthy relationship and it felt good. Although Mark and I initially agreed that we didn't want to be tied down in an exclusive relationship, but fate quickly turned the tables on us. After dating for about six months, I fell in love with him and thought better about telling him because falling in love wasn't part of my plan. Three months later, Mark asked me to marry him and I agreed because I loved him and thought we could have a good life together. Soon after, days turned into weeks before I heard or saw Mark. When I called him, he would tell me he was busy. Soon, I stopped calling, figuring out that he would call me when he had time. Weeks turned into months and then I never heard from him again. At the time, I couldn't afford to let my life skip a beat, so I continued working during the day, going to school at night, and pushing Mark to the back of my mind as far as I could.

Not too long after Mark and I lost contact, I lost my apartment in the Bronx and moved to a house in Brooklyn that my mother owned. When I was fourteen, my mother bought a three-family house in Brooklyn so her grown children could live there. The girls and I lived there as well, and during a brutal winter, the pipes froze and that made it impossible for us to continue living there. So, we temporarily moved back in with my mother in Harlem until the pipes in the house in Brooklyn were repaired.

While we lived with my mother, I continued dating when I could and on a night that I went dancing, I met another guy. I thought he was nice and we dated for a few months. But, it didn't take me long to realize that he was lazy and shiftless, with no real ambition in life. It took what I went through with Victor to realize what I DIDN'T want in a partner, so, I eventually left him alone.

Approximately a month after I left him and still in college, I found out I was pregnant. My mother was shocked when I told her. She really had a way of making me feel like I wasn't worth much as a human being and it was eerily similar to how she treated my father.

"I decided to help you with the girls because I figured you made a mistake by marrying Victor, but I'm not helping you with this one!" she said to me.

I prayed that one day my mother would get it. I was a grown woman with a job, two children and one on the way. But, this was one argument with her I wasn't going to walk away from. When I was young, I watched my father walk away from my mother on many occasions when she yelled, screamed and called him names. I didn't care this time if it turned into a screaming match and I was determined to speak my mind.

"Ma, the only help I needed from you was a place to stay because I had nowhere else to go. Although I appreciate the help you have given me so far with the girls, you never gave me the opportunity to ASK you for what I needed. You thought you KNEW what I needed because you still see me as a little kid, incapable of making decisions for myself. I am very capable of raising and taking care of my children on my own and you would have never tolerated ANYONE telling you how to take care of us. And, while you're standing there pointing out MY mistakes, why don't you pick up the phone and call Victor and tell him about his mistakes?" She was speechless.

For years, these were the kinds of arguments I would have with my mother.

It took me a while to get used to the fact that I was pregnant again, but it didn't last long. I took comfort in the fact that I was in a much better position financially by myself than when I was with Victor and had the girls. My pay from the City wasn't great, but it was enough for me to take care of the kids and me. Initially, I didn't tell my ex-boyfriend about the pregnancy because I didn't want a repeat of what I went through with Victor. I didn't want to be back in Family Court and I didn't want the drama in my life.

I had a change of heart when I was about seven months pregnant. I decided that he at least had a right to know I was pregnant and what he did with that information was up to him. After I told him, he decided he wanted nothing to do with his son and has never laid eyes on him. The pregnancy was taking its toll on me, so I dropped out of college. Derrick* was born shortly thereafter.

If I was going to achieve my goals, I had to make sure I didn't have any more children. Although I love children, being with Victor made me feel that being pregnant meant being in a position to be taken advantage of. And, I didn't want to be in a position where I could lose another child. I wanted to finish school and have a life so, shortly after I had Derrick, I had my tubes tied, cut and burned. PERMANENTLY. No more kids.

One of the supervisors at my City job was extremely encouraging and supportive when my son was born. I initially planned to go on maternity leave for about three months but she convinced me otherwise. She gave me some advice that changed my life.

"Don't take three months for maternity leave. The City gives you up to a year. Trust me, take it."

And I did. When I went on maternity leave, I used that time to my advantage. Through a friend, I heard about a very good secretarial school that was only nine months. that was all I needed to get back on my feet. I asked my mother to bear with me just a little while longer until I finished school. The relationship between me and my mother has been strained since I was a child and it worsened when I became an adult and lived with her. She felt I couldn't raise my children by myself and that I needed Victor and her around to help me or tell me what to do. A man had never abused her so she really didn't understand what I went through and how bad the abuse really was. Dealing with her was something I felt I had to do in order to better my life for my children and myself. A stepping-stone to something better. A means to an end.

Nine months later, I finished school, graduating at the top of my class with a GPA of 3.9. I was very proud of myself for finishing school, although it was not easy to go to school full-time and take care of three children. My mother on the other hand, felt I went to school to "meet boys." Not much of a surprise there. I tried not to let her negativity keep me from staying on a positive course. I did, however, land a good job as a legal secretary at a law firm making more money than I imagined. I felt positive about planning for my future because I wanted to get out of my mother's house and have a house of my own. Because Victor wanted to maintain control over me as well as have free access to me and the girls, he told the judge that he was afraid I would take the girls and he would never see them again. So, Judge Zuckerman issued a court order that stated I couldn't remove the girls from the jurisdiction of New York until they moved out on their own.

I couldn't afford to let that stop me from getting my own apartment, so I found a two bedroom with enough room for me and the kids. I enjoyed having my own space, paying my own rent and managing my own bills. More importantly, I had finally gotten away from Victor.

Victor thought he had beaten me, but one thing was for sure — he couldn't stop me from LIVING!

Coming December 2011!

*My Life, My Soul: Surviving, Healing
And Thriving After An Abusive Relationship*

Part 2: Healing

Sign up at www.mylifemysoul.com to be notified
when it will hit the stands!

About the Author

Ivette Attaud, a Harlem, New York native and former Fort Bragg army wife, has been a survivor of domestic violence and abuse for over twenty years. Having survived an abusive dating relationship and marriage to a Staff Sergeant in the Army, she managed to break the chains of her abuser. After years of extreme violence, abuse, a suicide attempt, a violent physical assault while pregnant with twins that resulted in the death of one of her daughters and a broken shoulder, Ivette left with her two surviving daughters and returned to New York.

In October 2008, she launched My Life My Soul, The Unspoken Journey of Life After Domestic Abuse.

Ivette served on the Battered Women's Justice Committee of Voices of Women Organizing Project in New York as well as contributed research regarding law guardians to their report *Justice Denied: How Family Courts in NYC Endanger Battered Women and Children*. She received a Certificate of Completion in Victim Assistance Training from the New York State Office For Victims of Crime; has received numerous awards for speaking at high schools and colleges; created and facilitated a domestic violence and abuse training for Chaplains called *Healing The Body Before The Spirit* and talks to teens in various high schools about dating violence and their internet footprint. She has also published an article in Spotlight on Recovery Magazine entitled, *Surviving the Loss of a Child*.

Ivette lives in New Jersey with her family.

Index

Made in the USA
Lexington, KY
12 December 2011